At a recent tournament, a man slipped his arm around my waist and said: "Tell me. How married are you?"

"Well," I replied, "My husband is my regular bridge partner. And you can't be more married than that."

cover by Tom Donnelly

How to Play Bridge With Your Spouse

...and Survive

by Roselyn Teukolsky

Foreword

by Dorothy Hayden Truscott

Published by Granovetter Books

Granovetter Books
18 Village View Bluff
Ballston Lake, NY 12019
(518) 899-6670

Printed in the United States of America
ISBN 0-940257-08-4

Contents

ACKNOWLEDGMENTS

I would like to thank all my friends for their inspiration and ideas and my so-called Panel of Experts for their unstinting bridge advice.

Very special thanks to: Dan Boye, Jean Boye, Bernie Gorkin, Mary Gorkin, Stephanie Heath, Elaine Kurasiewicz, Barry Passer, Don Probst, Debbie Subbarao and Suru Subbarao.

My sister, Brenda Cooper, who, despite a total lack of bridge knowledge, went through the manuscript with a fine tooth comb and told me in no uncertain terms what worked and what didn't.

My daughters, Rachel and Lauren, who provided ideas, advice and help with the manuscript.

Michael Lipkin, who suggested that I write an article about playing bridge with my husband.

Matthew and Pamela Granovetter for asking me, out of the blue, to write a book for them.

—*Roselyn Teukolsky, August, 1991*

Foreword

by Dorothy Hayden Truscott

I laughed all the way through *How to Play Bridge With Your Spouse . . . and Survive.* If Jean Kerr had been a bridge player, she would have written this book instead of *Please Don't Eat the Daisies.* Roselyn Teukolsky certainly writes a very funny story. Frankly, I wish I had written it.

And it's all so true. Tournament bridge is like a roller-coaster, where partners rocket up and down together from "euphoria" to "you-idiot." Unfortunately, when a married couple play bridge together, they tend to drag the marriage along with them, for better or for worse. Roselyn deals with everything from premarital bridge to bridge after the break-up. In any bridge event there is one winner and a whole bunch of losers, which bumps up the divorce statistics considerably.

What is the solution? How can a married couple play together and keep the marriage out of it? For answers, fasten your seat belt and read on.

To my husband, Saul,
who inspired all this.
♡♡

How to Play Bridge With Your Spouse

...and Survive

1

In the Genes: Hereditary Bickering

HOW TO MAKE A SERIOUS BRIDGE PARTNERSHIP WORK
IN A MARRIAGE. IS THIS A REALISTIC EXPECTATION?

ONE OF MY earliest memories: I am about two years old, and
perched on my dad's shoulders as he paces around the room.
He and my mom, who is sitting and knitting, are involved in
an intense, not entirely friendly, bridge argument. Every time
he disagrees with what she's saying, which is often, he either
whips around at 90 miles per hour to emphasize his point or
stops short in his tracks to regroup. The experience is thrilling
for me, like being on a defective rocking horse.

This was my heritage. My parents' verbal bridge battles
permeated my childhood and became part of my family
folklore. I was transfixed.

Soon after they were married, my father started teaching
my mother how to play. Our apartment overflowed with
bridge lessons. Many years later, when she had overtaken him
in ability, he continued to mastermind the bidding and hog the
hands. The following was typical:

Mom
♠ A K J 7 4
♡ 7 2
◇ A Q J 3
♣ A 2

West
♠ 3 2
♡ J 10 6 5 3
◇ 10 8 7 5
♣ 10 9

East
♠ 10 9 5
♡ 9 4
◇ K 9 4 2
♣ J 7 5 3

Dad
♠ Q 8 6
♡ A K Q 8
◇ 6
♣ K Q 8 6 4

West	Mom	East	Dad
Pass	1 ♠	Pass	2 ♣
Pass	3 ◇	Pass	4 NT[1]
Pass	5 ♠	Pass	7 NT

[1] fails to show spade support, masterminds the auction and hogs the hand, all in one bid.

West led a low diamond, and my father, reluctant to sink at trick one, played the ace. He now played the three top clubs, on the theory that if they didn't break, one opponent might be caught in a diamond-heart squeeze. This was not destined to be on the actual layout.

Notice that East *can* be squeezed in diamonds and clubs, but only if the spades and hearts are played first. My dad had to guess how to play this hand and he guessed wrong.

"I am the unluckiest player alive," he lamented. "I play the hand like a champ and I go down."

"Seven spades is cold," my mother said, "and you are senile."

Fighting

Every Saturday night they would have Couples Bridge, four couples who played teams-of-four, with husband-wife partnerships. The arguments would start early and gather steam as the evening wore on. I perceived that this was what my parents did for fun. One time neighbors in our apartment complex sent in the police to investigate the commotion. I remember everyone's utter astonishment when the embarrassed policeman came into our living room—they were, for goodness sake, just having a normal *bridge* game!

When I was older, and could accompany my parents to kibitz at the club, my observation of sparring couples was broadened. Not one married partnership that was amicable stands in my memory.

What hope, then, for me? There was never a time, while I was growing up, that my parents didn't fight at the bridge table. Their married friends, playing at our house, fought at the bridge table. Their married acquaintances, playing at the club, fought at the bridge table. I grew up steeped in the tradition of conjugal bridge discord, and was never given any reason to believe that things would be different for me.

Teaching

The stereotype of husband-wife bridge partnerships is universal. When I tell people that my favorite hobby is bridge with my husband, the reactions range from pity to incredulity, followed, invariably, by "How can you stand it?" or "Don't you want to kill each other?" or "My parents used to play bridge together, until. . . ."

The major question, then, is this: Is it possible, in the same life, to have a happy marriage and successful bridge partnership with your spouse? I look at the problems that are unique to marital partnerships and I wonder . . .

When you choose a bridge partner from the general (i.e., non-spousal) population, you tend to pick someone with comparable bridge skills. A major source of strife in husband-wife partnerships is a large disparity in abilities. This leads to tension: more frustration and heightened irritation in the better player and increased nervousness in the weaker player.

The potential for discord escalates when one spouse teaches

the other how to play bridge from scratch.

What if the learner has no flair?

What if the learner has too much flair and surpasses the teacher in ability?

What if the lessons continue without abatement long after the learner perceives the need for them?

And what if the learner starts giving lessons back in self-defense?

The setups as described are doomed to failure unless there is a conscious commitment on both sides to make them work.

On the part of the stronger player, exceptional patience and consideration are called for, qualities not often attributed to serious bridge players. Boorish behavior, distasteful at all times, is especially disgusting when aimed at a beginner. If you want to turn your spouse off bridge (and you), signal your displeasure by any of the following:

- Slam your cards on the table during defense.

- Laugh at partner's declarer play.

- Share the correct line of play with the whole room.

- Sigh with exasperation.

- Roll your eyeballs heavenward.

- Beseech the heavens (loudly) for guidance.

- And (of course) seek commiseration from your opponents at the table.

If you want your partner to learn fast (and who doesn't), offer encouragement and praise, without being patronizing. Note partner's mistakes for later discussion. Constructive criticism is fine, but don't be overly critical. Don't show off your expertise—"Too bad you didn't break up the squeeze with a spade switch, darling. . . ."

Remember, you too were once a novice, and you didn't

acquire your know-how overnight.

On the part of the weaker player, exceptional commitment to the game is called for. If your spouse is a serious player and you are serious about making this partnership work, the most important thing that you can do in self-defense is improve your bridge in a hurry. Study your bidding system with the same dedication that you studied your college courses. Make notes, read books by the experts and, yes, take note of what your partner says. Learn your agreements and stick to them. Be gracious in accepting criticism and, if sometimes it gets to be a bit much, remember that you are lucky to have a partner who is stronger than you. This will surely speed your progress along.

Bridge and Marriage

When husband and wife are roughly equal in ability—at least in the eyes of beholders—there are still many problems that are unique to married partnerships.

For one thing, if you are having a problem with your bridge partner, who also happens to be married to you, then you bring the problem home. What started off as merely a bad bridge evening escalates into an unpleasant drive home and culminates in an icy rest-of-the-night. No one wants to snuggle up to someone who spent the evening overbidding. On the other hand, that same bad session, played with a different partner, ends when the game ends. You can ponder the evening's tribulations on your own, reflectively, without the emotional trauma of continuing argument.

Another problem is familiarity with your spouse. We feel free to say things to one another at the bridge table that we would never say to a casual partner. We also know what words are especially hurtful to our spouse; therefore the hurt lasts longer. Long after the game is over, the lingering emotion is often remorse over how we fought, rather than regret for how we played.

Then there is the fact that any weakness in the marriage tends to be exacerbated at the bridge table. Think of these stereotypes: the hen-pecked husband; the know-it-all wife; the male chauvinist pig and faint-of-heart wishy-washy wife. Now picture these people playing bridge with their spouses! Not a pretty sight.

Finally, there just seems to be much more invested in a serious marital partnership than a non-marital one: huge chunks of time, energy and emotional involvement. Therefore, when things go wrong, there's much more to lose.

Making It Work

The problems have been posed, and the pictures painted are bleak. Can a conjugal partnership succeed? I believe that the answer is yes, if at least one member is committed to making it work.

Ann Landers receives scores of letters from women who are disenchanted with their husbands. Everything from dirty socks to pampered mistresses invades her columns; and Ann's advice is always the same: "Ask yourself whether you'd be better off without him," she says, "And then take the appropriate action."

What I'm suggesting is this: If bridge with your spouse has been choppy for a while, to the point where you don't enjoy it any more, ask yourself the Ann Landers question with respect to bridge. If the answer is yes, you *would* be better off without him or her as a bridge partner, do your marriage a favor and start playing with other people. New bridge partners are easier to find than new spouses!

If the answer is that despite your spouse's poor play, lack of judgment, free lessons, obnoxious behavior, insensitivity, etc., you are better off with him or her as a partner, adjust your attitude to make things work. Consider this: If you simply refuse to engage in argument, the argument will wither on the vine. Think positively. Take time to reflect on the reasons why this partner remains desirable above others. Is she a steady, dependable bridge player? Steadiness and dependability are rare bridge traits. Is he your best friend? It's great to share the thrills and spills of this roller-coaster game with your best friend. Is he sexy? It's fun to have a sexy bridge partner.

If the conclusion is yes, this partnership can succeed, but it takes effort. Bridge need not tarnish your relationship. In fact, it may enhance the positive in your marriage. By the way, after the next session of bridge with your spouse, don't flagellate each other over the bad hands. Snuggle up and talk about the good ones. Surely there were *some*?

2

Premarital Bridge:
Budding Partnership

HOW TO CONCENTRATE ON BRIDGE WHEN YOUR MIND IS ON SEX.

VERY SOON AFTER meeting the guy I would marry, it became apparent that he was ideal: he played his hands out well, generally returned my suit, and was flexible in the bidding. He also shared my passion for the game and got that fiery glint in the eye when discussing it. I won't say that it was love at first sight. However, after our first big win together at rubber bridge, his fate was sealed.

"Do you remember those outrageous college games?" I asked him recently. "When every hand seemed sexy?"

"You're crazy," my husband replied. "There's no such thing as a sexy bridge hand. In fact, some of the stuff you pull at the bridge table—take last night for instance—well, sexy is not exactly the adjective . . ."

· · · · · · · ·

Don't marry a bridge player," my mother said. "They're impossible to live with." However, I had simmered in a bridge stew all my life, and my future course seemed inevitable.

I have wonderful nostalgic memories of bridge and court-ship intertwined. With hormones and brain juices flowing in those early days, it was a heady time to learn bridge together.

Make no mistake, the bridge was always serious. Our foursome in college, disdaining more mundane activities like seminars and outdoor sports, would play for hours on end, punctuating the hands with long and ardent discussions. We tried to inject sense into the bidding. We insulted our opponents raucously. We dissected one another's plays with the ruthless precision of surgeons. We bandied about words like squeeze plays and endplays as if we knew what we were doing. They were delicious on the tongue.

Those early bridge dates with my future husband were fun. And yes, the hands were sexy.

North
♠ J 5
♡ 9 4 3
♦ A Q J 9 8 3
♣ 6 3

Me
♠ Q 9 7 6
♡ K Q 7
♦ 6 5 2
♣ K J 10

♡5

With both sides vulnerable, the bidding had gone:

Him	North	Me	South
Pass	Pass	Pass	1 ♡
Pass	2 ♡	Pass	Pass
Double	3 ♦	Pass	3 ♡
Pass	Pass	Pass	

My heart gave a slight lurch at the reopening double. Great spade support. Sexy voice. They duly took the push to three hearts, and I must say that defending this hand was effortless,

playing with the hunk across from me. His beautiful fingers
lingered briefly on his cards before flicking the five of hearts
onto the table. It went low, queen, ace. Declarer played a club.
Irresistible in every posture, he followed low, and I was in with
the jack. My partner uncrossed his long legs and leaned back
as I took about one second to ponder my next move: *he* had
led a heart, so a heart return must be right. I played king of
hearts and a heart, partner throwing a spade. Ah, his flowing
rhythm as he played his cards. Here was the entire hand:

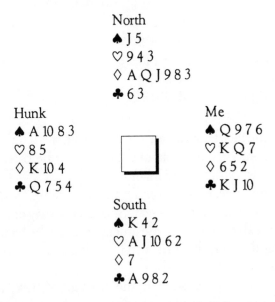

North
♠ J 5
♡ 9 4 3
◇ A Q J 9 8 3
♣ 6 3

Hunk
♠ A 10 8 3
♡ 8 5
◇ K 10 4
♣ Q 7 5 4

Me
♠ Q 9 7 6
♡ K Q 7
◇ 6 5 2
♣ K J 10

South
♠ K 4 2
♡ A J 10 6 2
◇ 7
♣ A 9 8 2

Declarer at this point finessed a diamond, threw a club on
the ace of diamonds, and, dejectedly, tried a spade to the king.
Sex and triumph mingled as Adonis produced the ace. One
more club trick and two more spade tricks, and it was down
two. Oh, were we talented!

I would like to believe that several years down the pike,
when the sexual fog had somewhat cleared, and I had become
less worshipful, that I would have defended this hand correctly
for the *right* reasons. That I would have given the intimidating
diamond suit in dummy at least a nervous glance. The beauty
of the hand lies in realizing that if declarer has as many as *two*

North
♠ J 5
♡ 9 4 3
◇ A Q J 9 8 3
♣ 6 3

Hunk
♠ A 10 8 3
♡ 8 5
◇ K 10 4
♣ Q 7 5 4

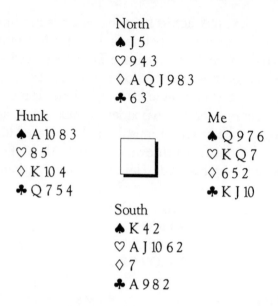

Me
♠ Q 9 7 6
♡ K Q 7
◇ 6 5 2
♣ K J 10

South
♠ K 4 2
♡ A J 10 6 2
◇ 7
♣ A 9 8 2

diamonds, the heart continuation is a disaster, but if he has less than two diamonds, the diamond suit cannot be brought in and the trump return is the killer.

Mike Lawrence, in his book "Dynamic Defense," leads the reader, who is in a defender's seat, through the play of a hand. Clues are piled up, until, at some crucial stage of the hand, one of the defenders has the lead, and it's make or break time in the defense.

For the sexy hand described, the moment of truth comes when I win the jack of clubs. At that time I have complete information. Using the Lawrence method (as opposed to the Adonis method), I might reason as follows. Rather than bid a suit, partner balanced with a reopening double, which suggests support for three suits. He must have three or four spades, and he has echoed in clubs showing an even number—four, to be consistent with the bidding. Further, the one-heart bid by declarer places at most two hearts in my partner's hand. Conclusion: partner has at least three diamonds and declarer no more than a singleton. The trump return is therefore right.

Notice that with the jack in dummy, a spade shift away from the queen is dangerous—declarer may duck it to partner's ace.

Declarer may now make his contract, if partner thinks you know what you're doing and leads a second round of spades to your presumed king. Declarer can now maneuver a spade ruff, a club to his ace, a successful diamond finesse, a club discard, a diamond ruffed in hand, and the last club ruffed in dummy. Making four.

A very sexy hand.

Bridge and Sex

Those were the days, when sex was the major feeling flowing between us at the bridge table. It was a time of shrugged-off disasters, cursory discussions and fleeting, superficial arguments that didn't matter. And all criticisms were delivered without the rancor that was to develop in later years. In retrospect I see that it was during those rosy days that we laid the foundations for future problems.

The sexual glow that embraced us at the bridge table created a buffer zone in which bad bridge habits could thrive. We were sexy and alluring. When either of us did something wonderful that worked, we became even sexier. We were loud and effusive about our brilliance. When things went wrong we gave instant lessons at the table. Usually it was *he* giving *me* lessons, since he was the more experienced player. This became an early feature of our relationship. The lessons in those days were delivered in a serious, polite, student-of-the-game manner. Perhaps he had figured out that being a boor at the bridge table was not going to make me swoon over him. The impressions we made on one another were still important. Being desirable at evening's end was still paramount.

How should you tackle the blood-tingling problem of concentrating on bridge when your mind is on sex? Some purists may argue that you should channel the energy into counting the cards. As I see it, there is just one sensible approach: enjoy the feeling while it lasts!

3

Newlyweds: Already Experts

♡♡

The way he gets me to smile at our wedding is to bid between takes. The photographer lines us up—grandmother here, Uncle Joe there—and then for the umpteenth time leers at us with "S-a-a-a-y sex!" My new husband whispers "Four hearts" in my ear, causing me to burst into laughter.

There is one great photo in which I am encircled by six of his aunts, and feel like a small white fortress surrounded by Sherman tanks. As I stand there, defenseless, I see him mouthing "Seven no trump" at me, which sets me off anew. In the actual photo I look like your everyday beaming bride. This wedding probably marks the last time in our partnership when he gets to bid and I don't.

The Joy of Conventions

The start of married life: long, glorious chunks of time in which to discuss card combinations and bidding.

Let's play this, let's play that: the investment of time begins.
Let's go here, let's go there: the investment of money begins.
Let's win: the expectations begin.

With marriage comes responsibility. No longer can we play by the seat of our pants, but need to implement some decent carding agreements and a revamped bidding system.

Goren's point count, which has served us so well up until now, will have to go. We discover the joys of five-card majors, limit raises and two-over-one game force. We read several books. We make copious notes. Our eyes light up at each new bauble for our treasure chest: Jacoby transfer bids; grand slam force; splinter bids; weak jump shifts in competition; gambling three notrumps; ad infinitum. *Everything* goes on the card.

But does all this bring happiness?

Him
♠ K J 5 4 2
♡ A 9 2
◇ A 7
♣ A 8 4

West
♠ 10 9 6
♡ J
◇ K Q J 10 6
♣ 10 9 6 2

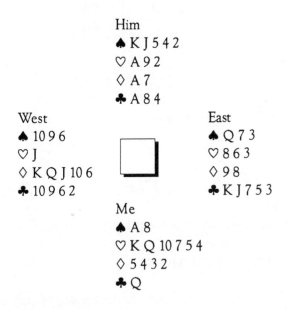

East
♠ Q 7 3
♡ 8 6 3
◇ 9 8
♣ K J 7 5 3

Me
♠ A 8
♡ K Q 10 7 5 4
◇ 5 4 3 2
♣ Q

This is from a Swiss team event against a very strong team. Everyone is vulnerable.

West	Him	East	Me
—	1 ♠	Pass	2 ♡ [1]
Pass	3 ♡ [2]	Pass	4 ♡ [3]

[1] Game force in the modern style
[2] Forcing and unlimited in the modern style
[3] The modern style leaves us both in the dark

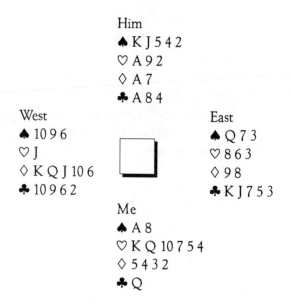

Him
♠ K J 5 4 2
♡ A 9 2
◊ A 7
♣ A 8 4

West
♠ 10 9 6
♡ J
◊ K Q J 10 6
♣ 10 9 6 2

East
♠ Q 7 3
♡ 8 6 3
◊ 9 8
♣ K J 7 5 3

Me
♠ A 8
♡ K Q 10 7 5 4
◊ 5 4 3 2
♣ Q

As dummy hits the table, I slump in my chair. We have surely missed six.

"Am I supposed to know you have this hand?" I ask. A rhetorical question.

"Play the hand," he says testily.

There's not much to the play. I win the ace of diamonds, cash the king of hearts, play ace, king of spades and ruff a spade. The suit comes tumbling down and all I lose is a diamond.

If I were in six, I think, I would play the hand the same way. If the queen of spades does not fall, my plan is to give up a diamond trick. If East does not return a trump, I can ruff both my remaining diamonds in dummy. If East does return a trump, I can win in my hand, ruff one diamond in dummy, and ruff a fourth spade in my hand. I can then draw the last trump, enter dummy with the ace of clubs and throw the fourth diamond on the fifth spade.

But all of this is conjecture. We are not in six.

"How could you not make a slam try?" I lash out after pulling in the twelfth trick. "Sixteen beautiful points *plus* a doubleton, and you bid like a wimp."

"You could have made it easy for me by bidding three spades," he throws back. "Your four heart bid denies the ace of spades."

"I *can't* cuebid with this hand," I groan, exasperated. "It's an *eleven*-point hand. I almost didn't bid two-over-one, forcing to game."

"You have to learn to evaluate a hand," he teaches. "As soon a I bid three hearts your hand escalates in value. It's a *great* hand. *Six* trumps, a *singleton*, the *ace* of *spades*." He grabs the napkin from under his coffee cup and scribbles furiously: ♠ x ♡ K J x x x ♢ K J x x ♣ K J x.

"*This* is the hand you showed me with your bidding. *Now* try making six."

"You're outrageous," I say. "I'd never force to game on junk like that." I am heartsick. We are so antagonistic. We have spent hours discussing our bidding system; that's why this seems to matter so much.

The experts at the other table reach and make the slam with apparent ease, and we lose the match by this one swing. We continue to do battle in front of our teammates, one of whom agrees with him, and one of whom is a friend for life when he concedes that it's a difficult hand.

We run around the room polling everyone in sight—"Who's to blame for this?"—but get no satisfaction from anyone. Several people tell me that they would not force to game with my hand. They would start with a forcing one notrump followed by a jump to three hearts. What is the matter with these people? Is it a conspiracy? Don't they see that if I had started with a forcing notrump, we would have had *no* chance to reach the slam? Perhaps we shouldn't be polling everyone in sight. What we really need is a Professional "Hot-Line" for bidding advice!

We go home drained and dejected. We came so close to winning this event.

· · · · · · · · ·

Our spirits are not devastated for long. Somewhere embedded in our psyche is the surefire knowledge that our game is on the rise.

We kiss and make up, and resolve to iron all the wrinkles out of our bidding system. These little misfortunes that befall us are temporary setbacks, stepping stones on the way to greatness. We have huge expectations from our game, and plunge with renewed vigor into uncharted bridge territory. Somewhere in the future, a big championship glimmers. . . .

Table Talk

There was never a time when we didn't feel we were experts, giving one another constant advice on play, bidding and defense. Without restraint. There were no arguments, really. These came later.

We spent so many hours discussing bridge in those first few years of marriage, that discussions at the bridge table seemed to be a natural extension. With the new familiarity of being married, we both felt free to comment liberally on one another's plays at the table. We never gave a thought to the fact that the criticism would become hurtful and, eventually, accusatory, thus detracting from the bridge and adversely affecting our relationship.

If there's just one piece of advice I'd give to new, married and non-married, partnerships, it's this: *Don't discuss bridge at the bridge table.*

Make this a rule early in your partnership because bad habits become ingrained and are hard to break later. For those who don't understand this concept, I'll elaborate:

- Don't discuss your partner's pitiful bidding at the bridge table.

- Don't discuss your partner's hopeless defense at the bridge table.

- Don't discuss your partner's pathetic declarer play at the bridge table.

If partner has made a mistake, he'll usually know it without having it pointed out in all its gory detail. If it's a subtle point, it needs to be raised when there's time to digest it. If it's a debatable point, it needs to be debated far away from the rest of the world!

Of course all poor results should be noted for a later, rational, preferably amicable, analysis; otherwise you won't learn from the mistakes. The discussion, however, should not take place directly following the hand, when emotions are running high and rationality is at its lowest ebb.

4

Postmarital Bridge: The Problems Start

HOW TO GET ALONG IN THE TENSE, COMPETITIVE
ATMOSPHERE OF TOURNAMENT BRIDGE.

"HAPPY BIRTHDAY," HE says to me. "What would you like?"

"A bridge tournament," I answer. "Preferably Hawaii."

Turns out, we're not really particular. We even go to tournaments in Buffalo and Scranton.

Another time, a colleague and I are discussing our summer plans. "Sounds wonderful," I lie, as she tells me about scuba diving in Santa Barbara/golfing in the Poconos/camping at Yellowstone/hiking in the Adirondacks/white water canoeing on the Hudson/helicoptering over the Grand Canyon.

"How about you?" she enquires.

"Well, we plan to spend ten days at the Chicago Hilton playing bridge," I reply, my adrenaline flowing at the thought.

"How nice," she murmurs. "Do you *do* anything while you're there. . . ?"

. . . .

So now that we've been married for quite a while, we've discovered that tournament bridge is what we do for fun. We hop from tournament to tournament whenever we can get away, experiencing the thrill of victory (occasionally) and the agony of defeat (often).

Our friends observe this quaint aberration of ours with bemused bafflement, but *we* understand it well. Tournament bridge is the ultimate roller coaster of exhilaration, despair, ecstasy, misery and frustration. On this ride we are inextricably bound together. When one of us plunges into the abyss of a disaster, the other is right there, sharing the darkness. And when one of us soars heavenward on the wings of brilliancy, star dust sprinkles us both. It's a miracle that *any* partnership, let alone a married one, can survive such emotional turmoil!

The intensity of the bridge experience has enriched our marriage beyond description. And it has bruised and buffeted it more than I care to think about.

Bad Vibes

Postmarital bridge is not as polite as premarital. Now that the marriage contract is signed and sealed, and we "belong to one another" in the Frank Sinatra sense, more liberties are taken in the obnoxiousness department. Tournament bridge has become serious stuff, consuming large quantities of time, energy and money. For example, we spend hours discussing count and attitude situations; so the blood rises fast when one of us misreads a signal. We debate our bidding system for days on end; therefore bidding misunderstandings don't make us feel too mellow either. Small wonder that we get angry and frustrated when the other blows it.

There's a tension now that wasn't there before. Sometimes during the defense of a hand, the horrible realization that I've played the wrong card grips me by the throat. I see that my feeble-minded failure to cover, or unblock, or ruff will soon be laid bare in all its awfulness, and my misery is augmented by the fact that when he realizes my error, he won't take it too well. His criticism is not exactly delivered in a pleasant tone of voice.

I have become resentful because I am much more forgiving of *his* mistakes. There'll be times when I note his poor plays on my card for later analysis, while continuing to smile sweetly. Then *I'll* make a play that *he* dislikes, and find that he doesn't show the same reticence about pointing it out to me. At times like this I want to strangle him.

He has found a new accusation to level at me: "You are unique. No one *in the world* would think of making the play you just made."

Well, I can add his underbidding to *my* list of grievances. A liberal in all aspects of his life, why he suddenly has to turn reactionary during an auction is a mystery to me.

He has become very hostile at the table. Especially when he thinks I didn't put enough effort into working out a hand. This hostility often manifests itself in not-so-subtle ways, like clutching his grimacing head in his hands. This is bad enough when I have, indeed, erred. The tension becomes intolerable when I think my plays impeccable, and *he* is the culprit. Words fly like poisoned darts.

My Responses

I, too, have my bag of tricks. I have several modes of retaliation. I get what he refers to as my "prune face," and freeze him out for the rest of the evening. Or I try to wound him by mouthing barbed-wire phrases and unprintable words at him. Sometimes I get up and leave the table while he's in mid-sentence. I threaten to make bridge dates with people he dislikes. (I once carried this through, much to my regret; my husband is still my best bridge partner.) And, my most powerful weapon of all, something that is terrifyingly self-destructive, but which punishes him beyond all other methods: I start overbidding.

It's taking longer and longer to make friends after a really bad session. . . .

· · · · · · · · ·

Hostile Hotshot
♠ 8 4 3 2
♡ A 9
◊ Q 8 6
♣ A 10 9 5

♡4   ☐

Me
♠ Q 6 5
♡ 8 5 3 2
◊ A K 7 3
♣ K 8

We were playing matchpoints, and I, holding the South hand, opened a nonvulnerable one notrump (12-14 points). This became the final contract, and West led the four of hearts, fourth best. I won the ace, East dropping the king.

At first glance it appeared to me that my only hope for making this contract was a three-three diamond split. Closer inspection revealed that I might be able to set up the fourth spade or score the queen if both the ace and king were with East. The problem with playing a low spade at trick-two was that if spades *didn't* break well and diamonds did, I might go down in a cold contract.

But wait! There was another chance. Suppose I played king, ace of clubs and the queen or jack appeared. Now I could play the ten of clubs, forcing out the other honor and setting up the nine for my seventh trick. I would hope that when they'd cashed their hearts, they'd guess to switch to diamonds rather than spades. If the spade honors were split, it might be unattractive for them to switch to spades. This line of play required a rosy, optimistic outlook on life. It appealed to me, because I thought that I might even make an overtrick if my club plays worked *and* the diamonds broke. Ah, the frenzied optimism of youth!

Of course, this didn't work. Here was the entire hand.

Hostile Hotshot
♠ 8 4 3 2
♡ A 9
◊ Q 8 6
♣ A 10 9 5

West
♠ A K J
♡ J 10 7 4
◊ J 5
♣ J 7 4 2

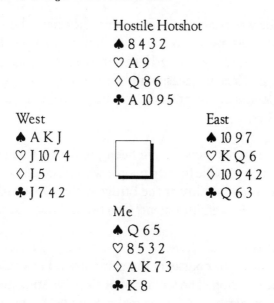

East
♠ 10 9 7
♡ K Q 6
◊ 10 9 4 2
♣ Q 6 3

Me
♠ Q 6 5
♡ 8 5 3 2
◊ A K 7 3
♣ K 8

My partner, from his side of the table, saw me play this
sequence of cards: ace of hearts; king, ace of clubs; queen, ace,
king of diamonds; followed by losing the rest of the tricks.
Down one. At about trick-ten, while my opponents were
merrily cashing their tricks, he started rolling his eyeballs and
shaking his head in disbelief. As if I'd lost my mind. Like I'd
returned to a previous life when all we knew was to cash aces
and kings.

"What happened to trying to make the contract?" he
snapped when the hand was over. "Like a spade towards the
queen at trick two?" Instead of dignifying this with a reply—
*the hand has only six tricks no matter what I do, you obnoxious
moron*—I mentally vaporized him, and took out the traveling
scoresheet. By that point in the session, two pairs had passed
the hand out and three had gone down one in one notrump.
A normal result, but, oh, the noxious fumes flowing between
us!

I later thought about the hand and saw that the winning
play at trick-two *was* a spade. West could cash three hearts,
but would have to make a great play—switch to the jack of
clubs—to set up a seventh defensive trick before dummy's

fourth spade was established. The point of the hand, however, was not whether my line of play was right or wrong—it was, in fact, naive—but that we had let a minor partscore hand ruin our evening. Thus, it occasionally happens that we actually win a single-session event, and drive home without speaking to each other!

. . . .

For quite awhile now I have been pondering these questions: How is it possible for two people who adore one another to generate such hostility at the bridge table? What makes it such a contentious environment? Can this marriage be saved?

The Tension
The problem, of course, is the game itself. For one thing there's The Tension. The feeling of one's palpitating heart as one observes partner trying to make a loudly-doubled contract. Sweating on the edge of one's seat when partner gains the lead, his turn to make the crucial defensive play. Make or break. It's now or never. Debating whether to bid that borderline slam in a close match. If it's wrong we will lose the match for sure. We sit in a bubble of tension. This kind of bridge tension is what makes the game exciting, but it invariably leads to *partnership* tension, which detracts from concentration and leads to inferior play.

A tactic that may help diffuse partnership tension is to inject some humor into the situation. Here are some ideas:

- Husbands and wives, especially longtime married ones, have hundreds of secret, intimate signals. After a poor result, try sending an intimate signal. . . .

- Another ploy that I use, once in a while, with some success, is the Irrational Kiss Technique. After he criticizes me for an unfortunate action, which, in my mind, was reasonable at the time, I get up from the table, and, with hatred and resentment welling up inside me, go plant a kiss on his head. It has, on occasion, rendered him speechless, no mean feat. The hardest part, of course, is getting myself to do it.

The Errors

Then there are The Errors. The people who win in this game are the ones who, in the long run, make the fewest mistakes. Bridge is a game of errors, and after all these years it's getting to be FRUSTRATING. In the old days we were much more inclined to shrug off errors because we weren't an established partnership. Now it all seems to matter more.

Reducing your own errors is one thing. Being accepting of partner's errors is the tough problem to deal with. Here are some tips for minimizing strife:

- Stick to your partnership understandings and agreements as if they were gospel. (Perhaps if I say this enough, I'll actually do it!) Don't deviate from making percentage plays unless there's overwhelming evidence that you should do so. Lame remarks like "I didn't think they'd double" or "She just looked like she was holding the queen" will not do much to mollify your partner.

- Work harder to improve your game. You'll still be frustrated, but at least your mistakes will be on a higher, less embarrassing level.

The Ego

Then there's The Ego. My Ego. Partner's Ego. Our teammates' Egos. Plus all the other Giant Egos of people who think they are Terrific Players (i.e., most tournament players). All these Egos get in the way of many meaningful bridge discussions, because the people who possess them don't like conceding any points and will argue until they are blue in the face about who caused a rotten result. No solutions here. Much as one accepts ants at a picnic, one must accept Large Egos as part of the tournament scene.

The Spouse Problem

Finally, and most significantly, there's the problem that tiny character flaws, small personality defects and slight mental deficiencies, which remain hidden for much of the time, become magnified a hundred times at the bridge table. *A thousand times if you and partner are married.*

- We're rude and ungracious in the extreme when one of us makes a mistake.

- Our intense irritation at partner always lurks just below the surface, and erupts at the slightest provocation.

- We make remarks like "You are *weak*," which often causes partner to be even weaker on the next hand.

- We lash out at one another, and then harbor simmering resentments over being ill-treated by someone who supposedly loves us.

- We become mentally obtuse and cannot comprehend the concept of no discussion of hands at the table.

- We totally reject the principle that later discussions should be in the spirit of avoiding future mishaps, not in the spirit of recrimination.

It is not clear that there are any solutions here either, short of dumping partner or telling him/her to get a new personality.

For my own part, I have used the Ann Landers Test, and am motivated to keep my husband as a bridge partner. He plays well; he is reliable; he is willing to drive to bridge tournaments. I have therefore explained to him, in a loving and rational moment away from the bridge table, how I plan to deal with the above problems:

- First, I will not argue with him at the table. Even if I feel unjustly accused, I will bite my tongue and say nothing. Even if I am provoked beyond human endurance, *I will not respond verbally.* I will write swear words on the card, next to the relevant hand number. I will open a book and read. I will get up and take a walk. Eventually he will have to quiet down, since even he will be embarrassed to appear to be talking to himself. I will put all my pent-up energy into concentrating on the next hand.

· Second, I shall try very hard to avoid the kinds of flamboyant plays that set him off. (How sad that partners in general, and spouses in particular, fail to see the humor in situations where brilliancy plays don't work!) At least in the immediate future I shall bid conservatively, avoid psyches and play by the book.

In short, I will try to make him happy.

5

Expecting Perfection: The Problems Continue

♡♡

HOW TO LOWER EXPECTATIONS TO A REALISTIC LEVEL
AT THE BRIDGE TABLE.

THE BANK HAS six large leather-bound catalogues of check designs. These include pages of astrological signs and two whole pages of golf clubs at different angles. I can also get sunsets, seascapes and grasslands. The checks come in most colors of the rainbow, and there are literally hundreds of different logos. If I like, I can choose checks that look like wedding invitations. Or ones that resemble those old maps in the illustrations for *Treasure Island*.

Actually, I'm not distracted by all this fluff. I am single-minded in my task. My husband asked me if I would order more checks from the bank, and I plan to surprise him with something a little snazzy, something that expresses our love affair with bridge.

·········

The aromatic roast beef and Yorkshire pudding are done just right, the way we all love it, rare and dripping with juices. Afterward, the Betty Crocker lemon cake is light and fluffy with just the right tang to the frosting. "You are marvellous," he sighs.

Our two perfect daughters, as far as we can tell, have turned out well. "They're gorgeous," he tells me 100 times a week.

I appreciate his work and listen enthusiastically as he expounds his theories of the universe. "You're incredible," he says.

"You're great," he breathes into my ear at night.

·········

The checks arrive in the mail: burnished ochre, with a tiny ace of spades, king of hearts and queen of diamonds fanned out in the top left-hand corner. He is amazed. "These are *perfect*," he declares.

This, then, is the great, unfathomable mystery of his existence: How is it possible that someone who has turned out to be perfect in Life, is not perfect in Bridge?

·········

Here we are, keen and intelligent, up and coming players, who read all the best books—*Master Play* by Terence Reese, *Better Bidding* by Marty Bergen, *Killing Defence* by Hugh Kelsey. Then we sit down at the table. We do not play like Reese, Bergen or Kelsey.

The Wife's Grievances
My partner's imperfections, are, for the moment, irrelevant. When *I* am less than perfect, however, he feels a pressing need

to straighten me out. His aim, it would seem, is to raise the level of my play to world caliber. Please understand, we are not discussing my major egregious blunders here. We are talking subtleties. Nuances. Shades of meaning.

For example, we'll spend five hours discussing a new kind of defensive carding, and then, joy of joys, it comes up successfully on a hand and we set our opponents three tricks, doubled. Does he say *Nice jack of hearts, darling?* Of course not. What comes out of his mouth is "You know, we can get it another trick if . . . *(you had been perfect)*."

I'll recognize a textbook situation and bring home a tough four-spade contract. Do I hear from him a *Nice pitch of the ace of diamonds, honey bunch?* Not on your life. His only comment is "You know, it's actually cold for five if . . . *(you had been perfect)*."

We reach a cold slam that *no one in the room* even dreams of. Does he find it in his heart to say *Wow sweetheart, what a bid you came up with?* Don't waste your time imagining it. All he can say is "Oh, were you lucky to make that! I'm not saying that we shouldn't have gotten there, but perhaps . . . *(you should have bid more perfectly)*."

Examples of My Imperfections

I am beginning to tire of his humorless approach to the game. Even when I play well, I am constantly reminded of my imperfections. I shall provide a few examples and let you judge whether I'm being overly sensitive.

Playing in a rubber bridge game at home, everyone vulnerable, I picked up ♠ A J 10 9 7 3 2 ♡ 5 2 ♢ 9 2 ♣ 7 4. My left-hand opponent opened three diamonds. My partner bid four hearts, and it went pass to me.

We do not preempt over preempts, so I knew that my husband was showing a good hand with at least six hearts. I paused to consider the hand. Our friends are solid citizens and play sound preempts. A bid of four spades looks tempting from my hand, but I was sure that my partner would play this as a cuebid, agreeing hearts, and that we'd find ourselves at the five-level or worse. "Pass," I said.

These were the hands:

Me
♠ A J 10 9 7 3 2
♡ 5 2
♢ 9 2
♣ 7 4

☐

Husband
♠ —
♡ A K Q 8 6 4 3
♢ 4
♣ K Q J 9 3

West	Me	East	Husband
—	—	3 ♢	4 ♡
Pass	Pass	Pass	

After I had placed the dummy on the table, he looked up at me and said "What took you so long to pass? You had nothing to think about." (*Translation: If you had even the slightest notion about bridge or bidding, you'd see immediately that a pass is automatic on this hand.*) I glared across the table and replied "Excuse me for thinking." (*Translation: You are such a slime ball.*) As you can see, not only am I expected to take the correct action—I must do it with no apparent thought.

Then there was this hand from a Swiss Team event:

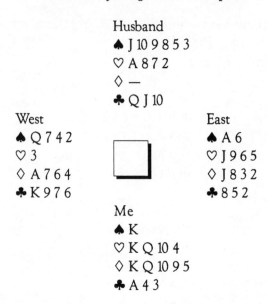

Husband
♠ J 10 9 8 5 3
♡ A 8 7 2
◊ —
♣ Q J 10

West
♠ Q 7 4 2
♡ 3
◊ A 7 6 4
♣ K 9 7 6

East
♠ A 6
♡ J 9 6 5
◊ J 8 3 2
♣ 8 5 2

Me
♠ K
♡ K Q 10 4
◊ K Q 10 9 5
♣ A 4 3

We were vulnerable, and, with no opposing bidding, I was declarer in four hearts. The six of clubs was led and, when the queen held, I played the three of spades from the board. East flew with the ace and, after much huddling, returned the eight of clubs. I won the ace and tried the king of diamonds. It went ace, ruff, deuce. I ruffed a spade back to my hand, pitched a club on the queen of diamonds, and proceeded to cross-ruff the rest of the hand. The lie of the cards was such that East had to start under-ruffing at some point, and all I lost was the ace of spades and a trump at the end. Making five, for 650.

Warmed by the glow of successful declarer play, I beamed across the table at my partner. He did not beam back. He had his serious look. "You'll probably make six if you lead the *jack* of spades at trick two," he pointed out instead. "East is less likely to go up with the ace." (*Translation: Yet again, you weren't perfect.*)

But East was having none of this. "I was playing the ace no matter what," he announced. Another perfect player. How can I deal with my imperfections among all these stars?

I suppose it's incidental to add that my opponent at the other table went down in four hearts. He drew two rounds of trumps before settling on a line of play.

One last hand will suffice to get all this off my chest. We were playing at our local duplicate game, and I held ♠ A 10 8 2 ♡ 8 6 ◇ K 8 3 2 ♣ 8 7 6.

I was sitting East and heard the following auction:

Husband	North	Me	South
Pass	1 ♠	Pass	2 ♡
Pass	4 ♡	Pass	4 NT
Pass	5 ♡	Pass	5 NT
Pass	6 ◇	?	

The North-South players were two very sweet ladies, who had learned bridge late in life and had not yet mastered the finer points of using Blackwood. Generally you should not bid five notrump unless the partnership possesses all four aces. Anyway, the six-diamond response seemed to present me with a golden opportunity to suggest a killing lead to my partner, and I doubled six diamonds. South converted to six hearts, and that concluded the auction.

After much crossing and uncrossing of legs, my husband dutifully put the jack of diamonds on the table. The sight of dummy warmed my heart, but not for long.

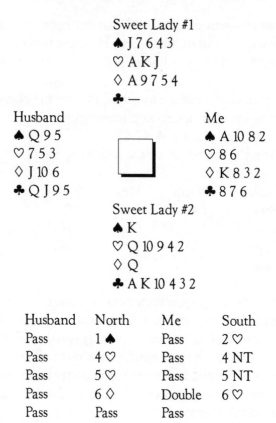

Sweet Lady #1
♠ J 7 6 4 3
♡ A K J
◇ A 9 7 5 4
♣ —

Husband
♠ Q 9 5
♡ 7 5 3
◇ J 10 6
♣ Q J 9 5

Me
♠ A 10 8 2
♡ 8 6
◇ K 8 3 2
♣ 8 7 6

Sweet Lady #2
♠ K
♡ Q 10 9 4 2
◇ Q
♣ A K 10 4 3 2

Husband	North	Me	South
Pass	1 ♠	Pass	2 ♡
Pass	4 ♡	Pass	4 NT
Pass	5 ♡	Pass	5 NT
Pass	6 ◇	Double	6 ♡
Pass	Pass	Pass	

Declarer called for the ace of diamonds, ruffed a diamond to her hand, ruffed a club with the ace of hearts, ruffed a diamond, ruffed a club with the king of hearts, and then called for the jack of hearts. She barely missed a beat before overtaking it with her queen, and drawing the remaining trumps with the ten, nine of hearts. When the clubs came down, she was home. All she lost was a spade. Well played!

My partner maintained his civil exterior until we had left the table, and then he turned on me and lashed out. "I wish you wouldn't do that!"

"Do what?" I enquired innocently.

"Make a lead-directing double when you don't have it," he said, karate chopping the air for emphasis.

"Why dear, what lead would you have made that would

have been better?" I asked, in the quasi-sarcastic voice I reserve for such occasions.

"Well, for one thing, if I lead a trump, which was my inclination on this auction, she has to be very sharp on the first trick, or else she goes down on the hand. Notice that if she wins on the board, which she may well do before thinking about the hand, she's dead. She can only survive a trump lead if she wins with the *queen*, using it as an entry for one of the club ruffs."

"And what makes you so certain that she'd make the wrong play at trick one?" I said. "She seemed pretty sharp to me. Since when are you the only one in the world who plays correctly at trick one?"

"Look, all I'm saying is what I've said a million times before," he persisted. "If you don't have it, don't bid."

"Do me a favor," I replied, thoroughly fed up. "Stop polluting the air with all this . . . *verbiage.*"

"No, *you* do *me* a favor," he continued, "Just practice saying 'pass.'" (*Translation: Don't ever make a bid that doesn't work.*)

I rest my case.

The Husband Responds

From time to time I peered over her shoulder as she scribbled away on this chapter; and in a sudden fit of even-handedness, she invited me to respond. I find myself turning around and leveling the same accusation at her: Because I fulfil all her expectations in life—believe me, I changed 50% of the diapers—she expects me to be perfect at the bridge table.

We have a wonderful bidding system, honed to perfection over the years, with so many cases in which it is absolutely clear-cut to pass. But no, instead of passing smoothly when these situations arise, what does she do? She practices psychological warfare on me by *thinking*. I die a thousand deaths waiting to see what she'll come up with. Then, when she eventually passes, she expects me to lie down in gratitude because she made the right bid.

Then there are the times when she bids with the expectation of finding specific, magic cards in my hand. Why is it that her wonderful, tempestuous nature must always manifest itself when she's bidding? In my opinion, she sometimes makes the most outrageous bids, violates our agreements, and then expects me to behave like a perfect gentleman when we land in ridiculous contracts. Despite the most extreme provocation, she expects me to say things like *Tough luck, sweetheart* or *Nice try, angel*. The way I see it is this: She attacks me with her bidding, then wants me to roll over and purr.

She has certain foibles that drive me up a tree. Don't get me wrong. She usually plays her hands out well, but once in a while she'll get it into her head to make an exotic false card—an "imaginative play" she calls it—that she hopes will deceive the opponents. Does she think we're playing against imbeciles? So I sit and watch the queen of spades go sailing out of her hand, for no apparent reason, and then when she goes down, I'm supposed to sit calmly, be perfect and say nothing. (Now, in her defense, it's true that she would have gone down on that particular hand anyway, but I wish she'd go down in the normal manner and give me some peace.)

She likes to believe that she has terrific table feel, and can *sense* who's holding what, and occasionally she makes anti-percentage plays based on these *hunches*. Even when these turn out to be right, I feel that I have to set her straight, because, in the long run, we can't win. She then gets irritated that I'm teaching her, even though we got a top. She makes a blatantly incorrect play, and I am supposed to pretend that nothing unusual happened, or, better still, *congratulate* her.

"Mark it on the card for later discussion," she tells me. Now I ask you. What would you do? I'm only human.

Some Tips

I'm not especially impressed by his feeble explanations. Nevertheless, I *do* have some tips for lowering expectations on both sides.

- If your partner makes a smart play that earns you a good result, be nice about it. Don't point out how he or she could have done even better.

- If a risky action turns out well, be gracious. Don't give a lesson on why the action was wrong.

- Accept the fact that partner is not a professional bridge player, and resist the urge to set him or her straight on every point, major or minor.

- If you make a dreadful blunder, or even a mere mistake that turns out to be disastrous, don't expect partner to behave like a saint. Accept the frustration that you have unleashed, and go on to the next hand without arguing.

- Try to be a little more perfect by sticking faithfully to your partnership agreements and understandings!

- Finally, just keep reminding one another that the price is right in this partnership. If you want a pro for a partner, go pay for one.

6

The Man Is the Captain:
Real Conflict

HOW TO DISABUSE HIM OF THE NOTION THAT HE CALLS
THE SHOTS IN THIS PARTNERSHIP.

I DON'T KNOW which bothers him more: my brilliant unblocking plays that allow them to make the contract, or my failure to unblock, thereby getting endplayed and allowing them to make the contract. But I *do* know what bothers him most: my failure to make a play that gets *him* off an endplay. Real Men don't get endplayed.

And yet, despite his Me-Tarzan-You-Jane act at the bridge table, I am assailed by a poignant memory.

I have just driven home after a long day at work. My elder daughter, three years old, is in the back seat. I stop by the mailbox, which is on her side, and, as part of a family ritual, I say "Will you get the letters, sweetheart?"

I watch the little fingers carefully lift out the letters one by one and pass them through the window. Today there must 15 pieces of assorted mail, junk or otherwise, and at this rate we will be here until tomorrow. It is late and I am tired. "*Please hurry up!*" I say.

The tiny hand stops in mid-air, and my child says to me, in much the same tone I sometimes use with her, "A mother should be more patient with small children." She pauses, and adds as an afterthought, "*Daddy* never rushes me."

While the letters continue their unhurried journey into the car, I reflect about Daddy. . . .

He ached for babies, and when they arrived, he immersed himself in their lives. He was the one they went to with their cuts and bruises, because he would kiss them better so beautifully, and use a whole box of band-aids to patch them up. In the matter of housework and childcare, we were equal partners.

Not so, however, in the matter of bridge.

. . . .

The way we met was in a little booth on my first day of college. He was sitting under a sign that said BRIDGE LESSONS–50 cents. Of course I enrolled, and then discovered that he and his hotshot cronies were the teachers. I had to learn fast, almost in self-defense, especially when they needed a fourth and condescended to let me play in their game. Despite the intimidation, I was an adept pupil, and by the end of the year was playing with my future husband on the university's bridge team.

Bridge and Shakespeare

That 50-cent fee bought me a lifetime of instruction. The evolution of our partnership has been much like the seven ages of man as expressed by Shakespeare in *As You Like It*.

52   *How to Play Bridge With Your Spouse ... and Survive*

All the world's a stage,
And all the men and women merely players;
They have their exits and their entrances;
And one man in his time plays many parts,
His acts being seven ages.

At first the infant. Mewling and puking in the nurse's arms;
In the beginning, I drank in his knowledge greedily, and then, obediently, spat it out on cue. In those days I accepted everything he said. In my mind he was the Guru who made no mistakes, and conscientiously guided me through mine. I would never would contradict him—I thought he was always right.

Then the whining school-boy, ... creeping like snail, Unwillingly to school.
Later, I was still his undisputed student, constantly shown the error of my bridge ways. But I grew reluctant in this role. As I gained in knowledge, I grew in independence. I began to have faith in my own bridge judgment and often found myself at odds with my mentor. Mostly, however, I was the obedient pupil and kept my mouth shut.

And then the lover, Sighing like furnace. . . .
I fell in love with him, and listened with adoration to every bridge criticism and nugget he threw my way. Our bridge relationship was harmonious in those days, and I seldom talked back. For many years he was the undisputed leader in our partnership. I was starry-eyed and didn't give his domination a thought. That was just the natural order of things.

Then a soldier, Full of strange oaths, . . . Jealous in honor, sudden and quick in quarrel, Seeking the bubble reputation, Even in the canon's mouth.
When was it that we entered this hostile phase, this great

bridge battlefield? Nowadays every auction is a minefield and every hand some kind of skirmish! Bridgewise, my husband is still living in the glorious past, suffused with the knowledge of his inalienable place as Captain of our bridge partnership. I, on the other hand, have moved into the era of Liberated Woman, and the result is a huge clash of wills.

My feminist sensibilities bristle at his In-this-partnership-I-am-always-right mentality. I resent his masculine lack of self-doubt. Somehow, without saying it, he manages to convey to me this message: If the little woman would only be quiet and listen occasionally, she might learn how to play bridge.

We have not yet entered the age of . . . *the justice, in fair round belly with good capon lin'd, With eyes severe and beard of formal cut, Full of wise saws and modern instances. . . .*
Help!

The Battlefield

We are playing in a Serious Duplicate Event when I pick up ♠ K Q 6 ♡ K 97 ◇ A 10 2 ♣ A 9 5 3. We are vulnerable, our opponents are not. My partner opens one spade, and my right hand opponent doubles. I redouble and it goes pass, pass, two clubs on my right. Now it is difficult-decision time. Should I double for penalties or should I make a forward-going bid to indicate slam interest?

I settle on the latter course and bid three clubs. My left-hand opponent passes, and my partner jumps to four spades. Another moment of truth. This bidding sequence doesn't come up that often, but we have a general understanding that when we're in a forcing auction, any jump bid indicates a minimum hand with good trumps. I should probably make a cuebid anyway with all that good stuff in my hand, but after much inner debate, I pass. The hands turn out to be:

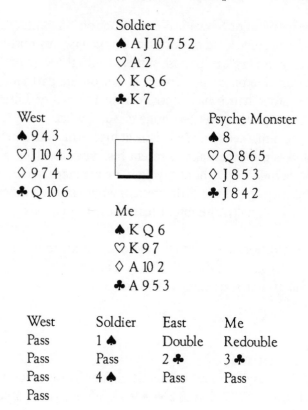

Soldier
♠ A J 10 7 5 2
♡ A 2
◇ K Q 6
♣ K 7

West
♠ 9 4 3
♡ J 10 4 3
◇ 9 7 4
♣ Q 10 6

Psyche Monster
♠ 8
♡ Q 8 6 5
◇ J 8 5 3
♣ J 8 4 2

Me
♠ K Q 6
♡ K 9 7
◇ A 10 2
♣ A 9 5 3

West	Soldier	East	Me
Pass	1 ♠	Double	Redouble
Pass	Pass	2 ♣	3 ♣
Pass	4 ♠	Pass	Pass
Pass			

When my partner sees the dummy, his face turns green, and for a second it looks like he simply won't recover from the sight of all that good stuff in my hand. Thirteen tricks are there for the taking. Without even bothering to state a line of play, he just throws his hand face up on the table and spits out at me, "Making seven."

The Argument

The fiery argument that ensues centers at first around the three-club bid. Then it escalates into the women's-rights and men-are-pigs arena.

"I cannot understand," he says acidly, "why you didn't pass two clubs to find out what my natural rebid would have been. Then when I bid *three* spades, the road to slam would have been easy."

"Well, *I* cannot understand," I reply with equal acidity, "why you had to bid *four* spades over three clubs. Three clubs is a game force, so why did you violate our principles and jump the bidding with a strong hand?"

He sighs and beseeches the heavens with his hands. How obtuse can one female get?

"Don't you see," he intones, talking slowly, as if to an idiot, "that the three-club bid was ambiguous in this sequence? For all I knew you were looking for three notrump. Or the best spot to play. It seemed clear to me that you could pass three spades."

"Oh, come on, don't give me that," I taunt. "Surely I'd go for a penalty double before opting to play in *partscore*. This is matchpoints, after all. Since when do we play that a cuebid of their suit is *not* forcing to game?"

"I also don't understand," he continues, ignoring me (typical!), "how you could fail to cuebid over four spades. Didn't it penetrate your skull that your hand was worth at least *one* slam try?"

"I've already told you," I respond, "that I interpreted four spades as a weak bid with no slam interest. I saw no reason to make a try, since I believed you the first time."

"Anyway, you obviously missed the point of this hand," he says (thump thump Me Tarzan), "which is that your three-club bid muddied the waters. You should have passed two clubs. Period."

"No, my dear, *you* have obviously missed the point of the hand," I retort, "which is this: my right-hand opponent made a great psyche against us and we didn't recover."

This sets him off again, as I knew it would. Real Men don't get taken in by psyches.

"You know what your problem is," he says angrily, switching from bridge teaching to psychoanalysis. "You're stubborn. You never concede, because somehow you're threatened by conceding to a *man*, heaven forbid."

"On the contrary, you arrogant lout," I reply "I don't concede because I think I'm right. Is it totally beyond your comprehension that you may be wrong? Hell would freeze over before you or your male buddies would ever admit that it was *your* bidding that caused a bad result!"

"Well, all I can say is, with your current attitude, you are never going to improve your bridge," is his charming parting shot. He, of course, needs no improvement.

I see what it is that inflames him: my defending my plays. He thinks he's the quintessential liberated male but gets worked up when his pronouncements are not the last word.

Male Chauvinists

I am not surprised by my husband's Man-Is-The-Captain complex. Sexism and chauvinism are rife in Bridge Land. I hear it in the macho postmortems of hotshot players; read it in the condescending articles about women bridge players; and see it in the way bridge organizations schedule women's events opposite open and major events. My husband has ample precedent for his attitudes.

When I glance about the field in a mixed event, what I see is a steamy jungle of roaring lions, chest-thumping gorillas and raging boars, all asserting their male dominance.

"You'd *better* make three spades doubled!" a wild boar roars at his partner, after she has pulled a close double.

"When am I going to teach you to lead trump?" a pig snorts, after an unsuccessful, but reasonable, opening lead from his wife.

"Don't show her your defensive carding," a grinning gorilla says to my husband when we alert our card. "It'll only confuse her."

"Don't *think*. Just lead my suit," grunts a small, portly hog.

"Listen, I taught you everything you know," says a large, hairy ape, in defense of his misdefense. "So I *knew* you didn't have a four-card major."

For the most part, the women partners seem to acquiesce in this mental subjugation, which then reinforces the male-superiority myth. Too many times I see a woman simper to her man after a hand—*Did I play the right card? Did I make you happy?*—and he, on his throne, King of the Jungle, looking down from a lofty height, pronounces his sacred judgment, eliciting the glistening tear of anguish or quivering smile of gratitude. I cringe.

I can speculate on the origins of all this. Little boys are raised to be Masters of the Universe and to display all the manly traits of aggressiveness, leadership, competitiveness and risk-taking. They are taught that the earth is theirs to inherit and grow up with a sense of their power and dominance as part of their birthright.

Little girls, on the other hand, are raised to be docile, gentle, and conscientious, and, of course, to look beautiful. They are taught that the earth is theirs to nurture and grow up with a sense of sexual power, but no power in a real sense.

By the time men and women reach the bridge table, their roles are firmly in place. Historically and culturally, men have called the shots. When they play bridge, they simply continue to do so as a natural extension of their lives. They are aggressive in their play and arrogant in their dealings with female partners. Their strategy after a poor result is to attack first. Women tend to be more docile in their bridge actions, less likely to make daring or imaginative plays. And in the matter of discussions, it seems that they defer to their men to keep the peace.

Obviously this is not *always* true, but I've noticed it enough times to comment on it. The Women's Movement has changed a lot of this; but the Women's Movement has not exactly penetrated the bridge world yet. The old traditional setup still dominates. Great women players still have a tough time gaining credibility in this bastion of male domination.

Gentle Castration Tips

How do you counteract a lifetime of upbringing, and disabuse your man of the notion that he is head honcho in your partnership?

· Let him know, in no uncertain terms, that you are not his student. You're willing to discuss hands, but you're not willing to be lectured on where you went wrong. If his urge to teach remains strong, let him open a bridge school.

· If he gives you an unsolicited lesson right after a hand—again, who asked him?—don't give him the satisfaction of agreeing with him. This will only reinforce his desire to teach. Ignore him. Compose a limerick. Get coffee.

· Later on, when discussing a hand, do not concede a point simply to make the peace. If you think you're right, put forward your arguments and agree to disagree if he doesn't see it your way.

· Consult other players whose bridge judgment you respect. My own self-esteem soared when I realized that experts were agreeing with *my* view about half the time!

· Do not *ever* give vent to your feelings with passionate or emotional outbursts. This will merely confirm for him that you are the Hysterical Female and he is the Cool Captain.

· Be a live wire in your partnership. Be independent. Read new books and infuse the partnership with *your* new ideas. Who knows, one day, he may listen to you.

7

Bridge With Another Couple:
Not Always Fun

♡♡ ♡♡

<small>HOW TO HAVE A FRIENDLY BRIDGE EVENING AT HOME.</small>

THE QUESTION IS whether to make the almond tart, which everyone loves, or the old-fashioned chocolate cake, which Henry would die for. Trouble is, Selena has recently developed a slight allergy to chocolate, which tends to become more pronounced when she plays bridge with Henry.

In a fit of indulgence I decide to make both. These will round out the dinner of grilled steak, salads and stuffed potatoes in the shapes of hearts and spades. Two bottles of chilled Blue Nun will soothe the passage through several rubbers of torrid bridge. Our bridge evenings at home with Henry and Selena are always lively, with food sometimes being the highlight!

They arrive early—more time for bridge—and present me with a gift, an apron, that says BRIDGE FOREVER, HOUSEWORK WHENEVER. We are all in good spirits. My husband got a hole-in-one at the golf course today, with three of his buddies looking on, so he's feeling hot. I swam several laps with my kids and cooked a four-course dinner, so I feel like Superwoman. Henry and Selena are starved for bridge.

The last of the steak has disappeared, and before you can say Marty Bergen we are at the table cutting for dealer. We always play fixed partners, we against them—very competitive. Henry and Selena have been married for several years and play together regularly in a fairly successful, though volatile, partnership. Henry also suffers from Man-is-the-Captain Disease, even though his wife sometimes plays better than he does. We are well matched.

The action is hot and heavy from the very first hand. They have an incredibly complicated bidding sequence that lands them in a grand slam off an ace, and we fail to cash that ace. The slam comes home. My husband, the great golfer, flips his ace at the ceiling and yells at me good-naturedly for believing their bidding and making a neutral lead; while Henry, the culprit, yells at Selena for believing *his* bidding and going for seven. I bring out the second bottle of wine, and we are off and running.

Later, Henry and Selena get their signals hopelessly crossed and allow me to bring home a vulnerable game that has no play. We win the rubber, and they blow up at each other. Selena's neck is starting to glow with red stripes and she hasn't touched the chocolate yet. Come to think of it, it's time to bring out the desserts.

And so the evening goes. We laugh a lot and yell a lot, but it looks like both marriages are going to survive. Then I pick up this hand: ♠ J 9 3 ♡ K 10 3 ◊ A 6 3 ♣ Q 7 6 5.
Nothing in it points to the start of World War III, so I am very mellow. I hear this auction:

West (me)	Selena	Golfer	Henry
—	1 ♡	Pass	4 NT
Pass	5 ♡	Pass	6 ♠
Pass	Pass	Pass	

What shall I lead?
The ace of diamonds seems clear-cut, and after a second's hesitation and a sip of wine, I lead it.

Selena (dummy)
♠ 7
♡ A 9 8 7 6 5
◇ 9 8 4
♣ A J 9

Me
♠ J 9 3
♡ K 10 3
◇ A 6 3
♣ Q 7 6 5

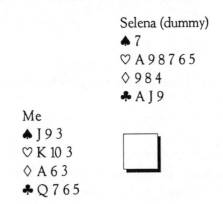

Henry glares at the dummy, glares at his partner, and mutters "I don't understand you." Ah, so the slam is not cold. On the ace of diamonds, declarer drops the queen. I continue a diamond, won by the king in declarer's hand.

My partner shows out on the second round of spades, and declarer starts running his suit. The first five spades are painless for me. I follow suit to three of them and then pitch a diamond and a club. Dummy lets go of a diamond, a club and two hearts.

On the sixth spade, I take a sip of wine. Partner's first discard was the two of hearts, a Lavinthal discard, promising club control. Thereafter he pitched three diamonds. I take another sip, and my tingling brain makes me cling to three clubs just for *one* more trick. I pitch a heart, as does dummy. Declarer is obviously not using dummy's heart suit. Another sip, and I part with a club on the seventh spade, as yet another heart goes from dummy, and also from partner. Here comes the eighth spade, and I tipsily pitch down to the stiff queen of clubs, as declarer pitches down to the stiff ace of hearts in dummy, and partner lets go of another club.

At this juncture, Selena is looking daggers at Henry; Henry is gulping down the rest of his wine and muttering to himself; and the golfer is banging his cards on the table, not a good sign. What's going on?

The last three tricks are: a heart to the ace, the ace of clubs, and the jack of clubs to my partner's king. Down one. Whew!

The Explosion

Everyone but me explodes at once.

Henry: "Since when is that a one-heart bid?"

The Golfer: "Your defense is something to be seen to be believed. You know that?"

Selena: "You are such an (expletive deleted)! You're pathetic."

Henry: "What's your problem tonight?"

Golfer: "You handed them this contract on a plate!"

Selena: "You're so obsessed with teaching me how to bid that you failed to make a contract that was cold after trick eight."

Henry: "Too much wine? Chocolate Cake? Menopause?"

Golfer: "I don't know why we even bother to play."

Everyone is furious. I don't have to be a genius to figure out that somehow my defense gave them the opportunity to make a hopeless contract, and that Henry failed to take advantage of my gift. We peer at all four hands so that we can torture ourselves all over again:

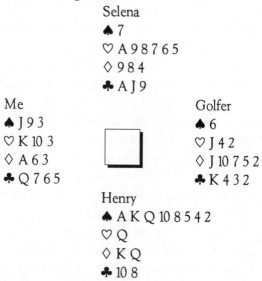

Selena
♠ 7
♡ A 9 8 7 6 5
◇ 9 8 4
♣ A J 9

Me
♠ J 9 3
♡ K 10 3
◇ A 6 3
♣ Q 7 6 5

Golfer
♠ 6
♡ J 4 2
◇ J 10 7 5 2
♣ K 4 3 2

Henry
♠ A K Q 10 8 5 4 2
♡ Q
◇ K Q
♣ 10 8

Selena claimed that the contract was cold after trick eight. Here was the position just before trick eight:

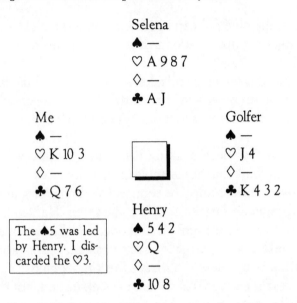

Selena
♠ —
♡ A 9 8 7
♦ —
♣ A J

Me
♠ —
♡ K 10 3
♦ —
♣ Q 7 6

Golfer
♠ —
♡ J 4
♦ —
♣ K 4 3 2

Henry
♠ 5 4 2
♡ Q
♦ —
♣ 10 8

The ♠5 was led by Henry. I discarded the ♡3.

And here was the position after my fateful heart pitch during trick eight:

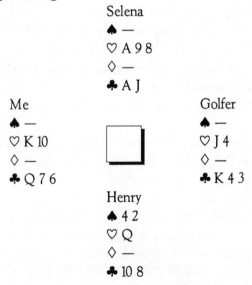

Selena
♠ —
♡ A 9 8
♦ —
♣ A J

Me
♠ —
♡ K 10
♦ —
♣ Q 7 6

Golfer
♠ —
♡ J 4
♦ —
♣ K 4 3

Henry
♠ 4 2
♡ Q
♦ —
♣ 10 8

"If you were half the expert you think you are," Selena says to Henry tauntingly, "you'd play ace of hearts and ruff a heart. You have nothing to lose. If the heart suit comes down, which it now does, the nine of hearts will be the twelfth trick! Why bother to run the stupid spade suit if you're not going to watch the discards?"

Henry is a defeated man and takes solace in more chocolate cake. "God you're unpleasant," he mutters through the crumbs. "Why don't you use some of that bitchy energy in learning how to bid?"

My partner has been shaking his head for the last five minutes, and I think that he resembles a ventriloquist's dummy with a broken neck spring. "As soon as I show out of spades, you should count declarer's tricks," he says to me. "He has eight spades, one heart, one diamond and one club. Eleven in all. You *know* he doesn't have the king of clubs, because he didn't claim at trick two. Therefore *I* have the king of clubs."

He pauses for his words of wisdom to sink in, and, just this once, they do. I see now that a heart discard from my hand was disastrous. "Notice that I didn't *rely* on you to figure this out," he continues sarcastically. "I made a Lavinthal discard to clarify the situation. Now all you have to do is hold all your hearts, I will hold clubs, and the slam has no play."

For once, I have no good comeback, mainly because he's right. But his sarcastic, unpleasant manner makes me belligerent, and I tell him to shut up.

"I think I'm tipsy," I say, offering a lame excuse to our friends.

My daughters are peering wide-eyed into the living room—they're after the chocolate cake. They know they've entered a minefield, and they tread carefully.

The evening fails to recapture its sparkle and earlier cheer, mainly because no one is especially communicative. Henry and Selena aren't talking to each other. I'm sinking into a massive bridge depression. And the golfer has been rendered speechless by my dreadful discard. We continue through two more listless, tight-lipped rubbers, and then agree to call it a night. We all say what a lovely evening it has been and smile bravely until they are out the door.

The Grand Irony

I reckon that in an evening we play over 40 hands, of which at least 30 are bid, defended and played without major blunders. Then there are another five, at least, in which errors are made, but the actions that people took were reasonable. This, then, is the grand irony: that it's the one or two bad ones that we carry home in our craw. That we torture ourselves with. That we ruin an evening with friends over. Why are we unable to recognize that it's precisely because bridge is such a difficult game that we keep coming back for more?

The evening always holds out such promise. Our opponents are good friends whose company we greatly enjoy. We always prepare terrific food for one another. The tension and competitiveness are always eased by an endless flow of tea, coffee, wine, desserts. And yet, we're even more sensitive to one another's errors than if we were playing in the World Pairs. Why are we, among friends, unable to laugh off bad hands? It must be because we all respect each other's games and our egos are painfully susceptible to bruising. I know that for myself, the worst tragedy in bridge is to make a stupid mistake in front of someone whose bridge I respect. That particular defensive error weighed me down for days!

How to Remain Friends

As I see it, there's only one solution to the problem of how to have an amicable bridge evening with another couple, and that's to rotate partners after each rubber, with each person keeping an individual score. This way, after a particularly trying rubber, you get relief: a new eager face opposite you.

It's a sad fact of life that we tend to be more polite to friends than to spouses, so this solution promises a more harmonious evening. What you lose, of course, are the non-negligible pleasures of using a familiar, sophisticated bidding system and being secure in your defensive carding. On the other hand, it is rather nice to be able to explain away disasters with the words *I'm sorry, that's not how I'm used to playing it!*

Or, you can always play *Trivial Pursuit*.

8

On the Beach:
Time to Revamp the System

DO NEW, ARTIFICIAL CONVENTIONS INCREASE
THE POTENTIAL FOR DISASTER?

WE ARE ON the beach, watching our two girls splashing in the ocean. As I look at these two little sun-loving, surf-loving frolickers, I think that they are surely throwbacks to some foreign ancestor. My husband, whose pale skin turns pink when you say the word *beach* in his presence, has come prepared. We have a spare beach umbrella, three bottles of #25 sunscreen, large ridiculous hats and Eric Crowhurst's *Precision Bidding in Acol*.

We are in the middle of our vacation at Cape Cod. Fifty weeks out of every year, our children must put up with two full-time careers, several bridge tournaments and gobs of Quality Time. For these two weeks in the summer, it is understood, though not explicitly stated, that we are their total slaves, committed to indulge their every whim and desire. Right now their favorite activity is jumping into the waves, with us watching and admiring. Seems to be a perfect time to add some gadgets to our bidding system.

Weak Jump-Shifts in the Sand

The first change we decide to make is to play weak jump-shifts in competition. At a recent Swiss Teams event, vulnerable against not, I held ♠ A 9 3 ♡ 8 ◇ A Q 10 5 2 ♣ A 9 7 5. The bidding went like this:

Me	North	Partner	South
1 ◇	1 ♡	Pass	3 ♡

The three-heart bid was explained to me as a limit raise, and after some internal debate, I passed. Partner could not have too many points and I was nervous about going for a number, doubled, at the four-level.

My decision turned out to be disastrous. My partner's hand was ♠ K 10 7 6 5 2 ♡ 6 4 2 ◇ J 6 ♣ 8 4, and four spades was bid and made at the other table. One of our teammates, not a great charmer at the best of times, made this remark: "If you can't reach four spades on these cards, then your bidding system isn't worth s—." I was stung.

Notice that if partner can insert a (weak) two-spade bid over North's one-heart overcall, we will easily reach four spades.

On the beach we toss several hands back and forth, and finally agree on these features for our weak-jump-shift hands:

• Less than six highcard points.

• At least six cards in the jump-shift suit, headed by at least one of the honors. In other words, with this hand: ♠ 10 9 8 4 3 2 ♡ K 7 2 ◇ Q 4 ♣ 9 7, we will bid *one* spade over a one-heart overcall, but with the following hand, we will bid two spades: ♠ K Q 8 4 3 2 ♡ 8 7 2 ◇ 6 4 ♣ 9 7.

"Mommy, let's get some ice cream!" I am being tugged away from the shady haven of our umbrella. Like Bedouins traversing the Arabian Desert, we set off across the hot sands. I feel good about our new understanding—not only can we reach these close games now, but I see great scope for preempting our opponents out of *their* best spot.

Sand Castles and Minor-Suit Swiss

The next morning, I am building the moat, and my husband is using empty ice cream cups to do some fancy architecture on the main towers. My girls are racing back and forth with their pails, fetching water to fill the moat. This is a sand castle de luxe.

Eventually they are back in the ocean, and we are back in the safety of our deck chairs, leafing through Crowhurst. We don't play Acol, but this book has been recommended to us as one that has outstanding bidding ideas, and we've not been disappointed. Today we will add Minor-Suit Swiss to our arsenal.

Minor-Suit Swiss provides a way of showing a strong minor-suit raise, with or without a four-card major. Thus, if partner opens one diamond and you hold: ♠ K Q 7 2 ♡ A 8 7 ◇ K Q 9 8 ♣ J 10, you bid *three* spades, guaranteeing 13-15 points, at least four diamonds and exactly four spades. Over this bid, partner's options are:

· Three notrump = no interest in slam.

· Four diamonds = interest in a diamond slam; invites cuebidding.

· Any other suit = cuebid agreeing spades.

· Four notrump = forcing; invites partner to bid either six diamonds, or six notrump with a maximum.

Suppose your hand is ♠ K 10 ♡ A J 9 2 ◊ 3 ♣ A 10 9 7 5 2, and partner opens one ₊club. Bid three hearts, Minor-Suit Swiss. If partner now bids three notrump, bid four clubs (I really have a terrific club hand. Are you sure there's no slam?) Now a bid of four notrump by partner is sign-off.

The following aspect of this convention is useful if you don't play forcing minor-suit raises. If your partner opens one of a minor, and you have 13-15 points, at least four-card support for the minor and *no* four-card major, you describe this hand by bidding three of the other minor.

For example, if partner opens one club, and you hold ♠ A 6 2 ♡ K J 8 ◊ K 3 ♣ A 7 6 4 3, you bid three diamonds. With no interest in a club slam, partner will sign off in three notrump. Any other bid is a cuebid agreeing clubs.

I love this convention, and happily add it to our card.

The Aquarium and Stayman in Doubt

It is the next day, and with 30 mile-per-hour gusts, and intermittent rain, we are being treated to the fickleness of New England weather. We decide to visit an aquarium, which, much to my horror and my children's delight, has a duck that plays the piano when you put 25 cents in the slot. This is an unusual aquarium in more ways than one: it also has a large petting zoo, where we are obliged to spend over an hour in the company of all sorts of unwholesome-smelling creatures. While the girls pet the animals, we explore more Crowhurst.

We find an extremely attractive convention called Stayman in Doubt (SID). After hearing two-of-a-major bid in response to Stayman, the two-club bidder now bids three diamonds, a further inquiry about the notrumper's hand. With 4-3-3-3 distribution, the response is three notrump. This enables the partnership to play in three notrump, often a better contract than four-of-the-major, if both hands are flat. If the one-notrump opening bidder *has a doubleton* somewhere, there are three choices of responses:

- Three of the major = poor trump quality.

    •

- Four of the major = good trump quality and a minimum hand.

- Cuebid of another suit = good trump quality and a maximum hand.

This convention is especially useful in evaluating 15-16 point hands opposite partner's 15-17 one notrump. For example, suppose you hold ♠ A 8 7 2 ♡ K 7 3 ◇ A Q 4 ♣ K 8 2, and hear your partner open a 15-17 point notrump. You bid two clubs, Stayman, and partner responds two spades. You now bid three diamonds, SID, asking partner to clarify his hand.

If partner bids three notrump, showing 4-3-3-3 distribution, you pass. If you're playing matchpoints, you'll probably get a good score just for being in notrump. Don't risk slam. Partner rates to have something like this:
♠ K Q 5 4 ♡ A 9 2 ◇ K 7 2 ♣ A 6 4.

If partner bids three spades, showing poor trump quality and a doubleton, be content to play in four spades. You rate to have two trump losers. Here is a typical hand for this bid:
♠ Q 6 5 4 ♡ A 9 ◇ K 7 2 ♣ A Q J 4.

If partner responds four spades, showing a minimum hand, good trumps and a doubleton, you know that slam will be close. It may need some luck to bring it home. Other factors come into play here. Is this a close match against a strong team? Do you need a board to win a matchpoint event? Then go for it! Partner rates to hold something like:
♠ K Q 5 4 ♡ Q 9 ◇ K 7 2 ♣ A J 6 4.

Finally, if partner bids four clubs, showing a maximum hand, a doubleton, good trumps and first round control of clubs, slam looks like a good bet. Partner is promising something like ♠ K Q 5 4 ♡ A 9 ◇ K 7 2 ♣ A 7 6 4.

SID is such a nice convention, it's made me feel good all

over. I have the sense of a day well spent, despite the weather.

Back to Reality

We return home all pumped up, ready to set the bridge world on fire with our hot new conventions. On the very first night back at the club, on the very first hand, I pick up as South: ♠ K Q 3 ♡ K Q 10 4 ◊ A K 9 4 2 ♣ 3.

No one is vulnerable, I am in first seat and I open one diamond. West overcalls two clubs, and my partner bids *three* spades. Alert! Nobody asks me what the bid means, and the auction proceeds as follows:

Me	West	Partner	East
1 ◊	2 ♣	3 ♠	Pass
4 ◊	Pass	4 ♠	Pass
6 ◊	Double	Pass	Pass
Pass			

My partner has his baffled, why-does-she-do-this-to-me look, and my left-hand opponent is acting like John Wayne in the saddle. Without a second's hesitation, he leads face down, and his partner asks me what I think my partner has.

Extremely pleased with our new convention, I explain that the three-spade bid is Minor-Suit Swiss, and that my partner is showing 13-15 points, at least four diamonds and exactly four spades. The four-spade bid is a cuebid accepting my slam invitation.

West shrugs, and turns over the ace of hearts, while my partner, looking like someone who has just swallowed castor oil, tables this hand: Surprise!

Partner's dummy

♠ A 10 8 6 4 2
♡ 8
◊ 7 5
♣ 6 5 4 2

Nailed Down in Blood

Oh no! This isn't happening. Are we in the same room? Are we on the same hand? Where did Minor Suit Swiss go?

"My bid was a weak-jump shift in competition," my partner informs me acidly. "Over the two-club overcall, three spades is a *single* jump."

My heart is in my shoes. It simply didn't occur to me that the bid wasn't Minor Suit Swiss. There's nothing to discuss or argue about. This was a straightforward bidding accident, caused by all our new conventions.

There's not much to the play of this hand. My left-hand opponent shows up with both missing aces and the queen third of trumps, so I go down two. Too sad. A shroud of gloom descends on us and our new, revamped bidding system.

Later, when we have bounced back and are already thinking Next Event, we discuss this hand. We agree that the weak jump-shift will always take precedence over Minor Suit Swiss, since a cuebid of the opponents' suit is available for strong hands. On hands where there is no ambiguity, for example: one diamond – one heart overcall, followed by three spades, we decide that three spades will be Minor Suit Swiss *and* will guarantee a heart stopper. Without a heart stopper and any opening hand or better, we will simply cuebid our opponent's suit. It would seem that this convention has been nailed down, in blood, at the table!

Our Friend SID

SID, Stayman in Doubt, does not put in an appearance for several weeks. Suddenly one night it comes up, and we use it successfully to avoid a bad 31-point slam. Turns out that *every other pair* at our club, without the benefit of our friend SID, stays out of slam, too! I ask myself if we're better off because *we* stayed out confidently?

Increasing Potential For Disaster

Here is a burning question: Given that bridge with my

husband is such a volatile endeavor, do we just increase the potential for disaster by adding exotic, artificial conventions to our bidding system? Wouldn't life be simpler and more harmonious if we kept artificial bids to a minimum?

After much deliberation, I've decided that without conventions, the potential for dramatic disasters, like the one described above, would be lowered, but in the long run, we'd reach the right contract less often. Therefore, assuming that we have the fortitude to survive the occasional massive bidding misunderstanding, it seems worthwhile to persevere with new conventions that we judge to be valuable. I feel that we should capitalize on the plentiful hours that marriage provides to discuss each new convention. Let's face it— adding new gadgets to your arsenal improves your bidding in the long run, and makes the bidding aspect of bridge considerably more interesting!

Minimizing Misunderstandings

Suppose you decide to go along with the crazy notion that artificial bids are beneficial to your partnership, and you charge off to add Colorful Cuebids, Marty Bergen's Two Under Preempts, South African Transfers, and many more to your card. All of these are surely a dozen disasters waiting to happen. How can you minimize the risks?

- Don't get carried away. Even though the lure of exciting new bids is irresistible, you should not add more than one new convention to your card at a time. This way, you allow each addition to settle in and become part of your bloodstream.

- Don't add a new convention at the table. Add it before the session or after the session, but never in the middle of the session. If something comes up that you want to change, agree on the change for *next time*.

- Be sure to discuss how you will treat each new convention

over interference. The accident described in this chapter was totally avoidable. We should have foreseen the ambiguity that could arise in the given situation.

· Keep a notebook describing each artificial bid and convention you play. If your marriage manages to survive your bridge partnership, chances are you will have built up quite a collection over the years!

· Review your notebook from time to time! Preferably before an important tournament. Some conventions come up, if you're lucky, once every ten years. You want to be sure that at the moment of truth you *remember* that four diamonds asks you to cuebid a singleton or void, and is *not* a run-out to diamonds! (Yes, this is what we play over partner's gambling three notrump opening bid!) What a tragedy to spend 25 hours in 1965 discussing something wonderful and then having one of you forget it when it comes up in 1985!

· Finally, keep cool if you *do* have a misunderstanding. Just be aware that this is part of the price you pay for improving your bidding system. Comfort yourself with the thought that there's nothing like a full-blown, catastrophic misunderstanding for nailing down a new convention. You probably won't make the same mistake twice!

9

At the Supermarket:
Bridge Among the Broccoli

How to improve your bridge in strange places.

During the weekly shopping, something in the vegetable section reminds him of a hand I played last night. It has obviously been with him through oranges, grapefruits, apples and bananas, and finally comes together near the broccoli.

"Remember the seven notrump hand?" he says to me, loading a wilted head of broccoli into the cart. "I think you could have played it better."

"Yes, I remember the hand," I say defensively, "and I think *you* could have bid it better."

"What are you talking about?" he protests, lightly whacking me with a lettuce, "I bid it beautifully. I avoided a tortured auction!"

As I poke through the onions, I mentally start replaying the hand.

Him
♠ K 5 4
♡ A Q 7 2
◇ 3 2
♣ A 10 9 3

♠ J   ☐

Me
♠ A Q 7 2
♡ K 10
◇ A K Q 6
♣ K Q 4

West	Him	East	Me
—	—	—	2 ♣
Pass	2 ◇	Pass	2 NT
Pass	7 NT		

The jack of spades was led, and I added up 12 tricks. Lots of chances for a thirteenth—for example, if either black suit split three-three (in the next life) or if the jack of clubs dropped. Or if I could somehow maneuver a squeeze. Trouble was, there were so many menaces in the hand, I wasn't sure what to use as squeeze cards!

Anyway, being an optimist, I started out by cashing three spades. East discarded a diamond on the third spade. I then played the ace, king, queen of diamonds, West pitching a heart. On the queen of diamonds, I too pitched a heart. Now I played king, ace, queen of hearts. On the third heart, West threw a club, while I discarded a diamond from my hand.

Here was the information I had gathered so far: East had started with two spades, four hearts and five diamonds. He therefore could have no more than two clubs. My contract was cold! I could now cash the king, queen of clubs and finesse a club if necessary. I didn't have to bother. On the third club, the jack appeared from West, whom I had inadvertently squeezed in the black suits.

The entire deal was:

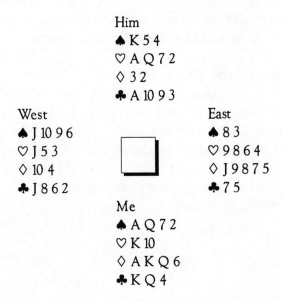

Here was the five-card ending, just before I cashed the queen of hearts:

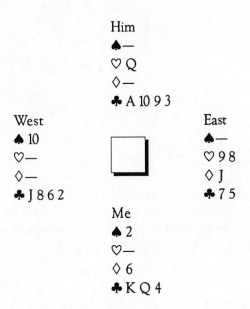

Notice that if I discard the spade instead of the diamond, West can ditch his spade and is no longer squeezed. This might bring him a rush of happiness, but it will be short-lived: I know enough about the hand to finesse his jack of clubs.

Bridge Among the Chicken Livers

We are at the meat counter waiting for the butcher's assistant to check for chicken livers in the back.

"I'm not sure that your line would have worked if the East and West hands had been interchanged," my intrepid husband says. He grabs one of the paper towels reserved for leaky meat packages, and scribbles furiously. In a minute we are both peering intently at this layout:

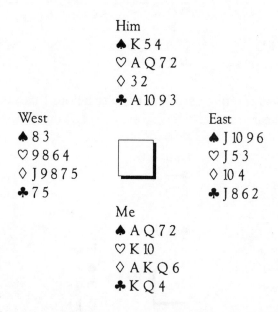

Him
♠ K 5 4
♡ A Q 7 2
◊ 3 2
♣ A 10 9 3

West
♠ 8 3
♡ 9 8 6 4
◊ J 9 8 7 5
♣ 7 5

East
♠ J 10 9 6
♡ J 5 3
◊ 10 4
♣ J 8 6 2

Me
♠ A Q 7 2
♡ K 10
◊ A K Q 6
♣ K Q 4

"My line still works!" I screech in triumph. "Remember—three spades, followed by three diamonds, followed by three hearts. The third heart will squeeze East in clubs and spades." Just to rub it in, I jot down the five-card ending:

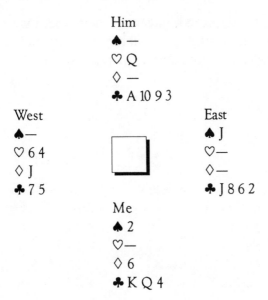

Him
♠ —
♡ Q
◇ —
♣ A 10 9 3

West
♠—
♡ 6 4
◇ J
♣ 7 5

East
♠ J
♡—
◇—
♣ J 8 6 2

Me
♠ 2
♡—
◇ 6
♣ K Q 4

On the play of the queen of hearts, if East keeps his clubs, my thirteenth trick will be the deuce of spades. "Nifty, huh?" I am pretty pleased with myself.

But he is not deterred. Brandishing the container of livers, he continues: "You just happened to luck out with this particular distribution."

"How lucky can one get?" I interject, sarcastically. "I mean, the black suits broke like a dream."

"Wait, let me finish," he persists, as we trot down the aisles. "The way you played it—pitching a heart on the third diamond—you gave up on using the heart suit as a menace."

I start to listen carefully. Sometimes, he knows what he's talking about, especially if the speech is delivered in amicable surroundings.

Bridge Among the Cheese

We arrive at the Cheese Carousel and he's still going strong: "Surely it's right to play off three rounds of spades, followed by three rounds of *clubs*, so that you can see what they discard before *you* have to discard. If both of your black menaces are well placed—meaning their length is situated under your length—then you will have an automatic double squeeze." He is still clutching the paper towel, and scribbles again.

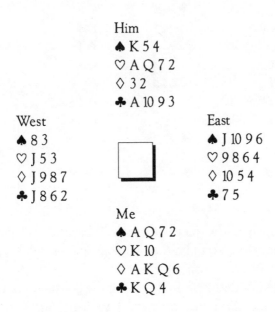

Him
♠ K 5 4
♡ A Q 7 2
◇ 3 2
♣ A 10 9 3

West
♠ 8 3
♡ J 5 3
◇ J 9 8 7
♣ J 8 6 2

East
♠ J 10 9 6
♡ 9 8 6 4
◇ 10 5 4
♣ 7 5

Me
♠ A Q 7 2
♡ K 10
◇ A K Q 6
♣ K Q 4

"Perfect position of black menaces," he says. "Assuming that three rounds each of spades and clubs have been played, notice that playing hearts next squeezes West. Or, if you want to sock it to East, play diamonds next. It doesn't matter."

"You're right." I say sweetly, "although, of course, West did lead the jack of spades, which suggests he has the spade length." I pause to let that sink in, then: "Besides, my line works on this layout, too. West gets squeezed."

He grunts, loads the extra sharp cheddar, and pauses for a while. I can see that he's groping in his mind for a distribution that will prove his point, preferably one in which my line of play doesn't work. I don't have to wait long. Scribble, scribble.

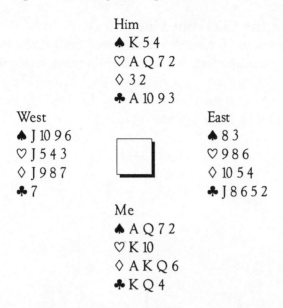

Him
♠ K 5 4
♡ A Q 7 2
♢ 3 2
♣ A 10 9 3

West
♠ J 10 9 6
♡ J 5 4 3
♢ J 9 8 7
♣ 7

East
♠ 8 3
♡ 9 8 6
♢ 10 5 4
♣ J 8 6 5 2

Me
♠ A Q 7 2
♡ K 10
♢ A K Q 6
♣ K Q 4

He forges on ahead. "Watch what happens on my line of playing six black cards first. West must throw two red cards. Suppose he throws diamonds. You now play diamonds, and your thirteenth trick will be the six of diamonds. If he throws hearts, you will play hearts and will score the thirteenth trick with a heart.

"Now look what happens in your line of play. West will follow to three rounds of spades and three rounds of diamonds. When he sees you pitch a heart, he will breathe a huge sigh of relief, because the pressure is off. He can now happily throw hearts on your clubs and sit back and wait for the setting trick."

My exuberance is somewhat subdued by his logic, and I absentmindedly add Feathered Friends Bird Food to our cart. This hand intrigues me more and more. As we approach the checkout line, I decide to look at all the permutations of distributions of East-West hands that do not include three-three breaks of either black suit. I am motivated by both curiosity and feistiness—will his line of play *really* work more times than mine? Certainly what he says makes sense.

Bridge in the Checkout Line

We examine all combinations where each defender has length in two suits, such as 4-4-3-2 distributions, or where one defender guards three suits, such as 4-4-4-1 hands. The results are amazing—this slam is cold most of the time! We find *just one* case in which neither line works.

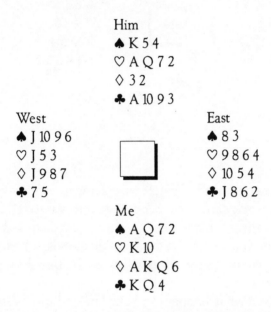

```
                         Him
                         ♠ K 5 4
                         ♡ A Q 7 2
                         ◊ 3 2
                         ♣ A 10 9 3
      West                                East
      ♠ J 10 9 6                          ♠ 8 3
      ♡ J 5 3                             ♡ 9 8 6 4
      ◊ J 9 8 7                           ◊ 10 5 4
      ♣ 7 5                               ♣ J 8 6 2
                         Me
                         ♠ A Q 7 2
                         ♡ K 10
                         ◊ A K Q 6
                         ♣ K Q 4
```

We stare at all four hands, but cannot find any way to take thirteen tricks, assuming best defense. Notice that every menace is badly placed.

Now for the really wild part. It transpires that my line of play is "better" than his in the sense that it works more often! We discover a problem with his line in all the 4-4-4-1 hands that include four clubs and four spades. The line may fail because declarer has to guess which red suit to play first. If he guesses wrong, namely he does not play the suit that has the singleton, he cannot recover, since he will lack entries back to his menaces.

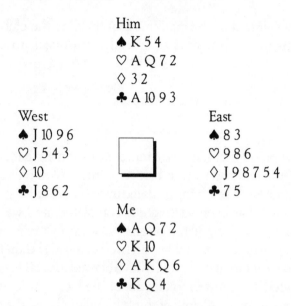

Him
♠ K 5 4
♡ A Q 7 2
◊ 3 2
♣ A 10 9 3

West
♠ J 10 9 6
♡ J 5 4 3
◊ 10
♣ J 8 6 2

East
♠ 8 3
♡ 9 8 6
◊ J 9 8 7 5 4
♣ 7 5

Me
♠ A Q 7 2
♡ K 10
◊ A K Q 6
♣ K Q 4

Observe the effect of cashing six black cards first. West will follow suit to all of them and declarer must guess which red suit to play next. If he guesses hearts, he will go down, because on the run of the diamonds West can now comfortably part with his fourth heart and fourth club; declarer is cut off from dummy forever.

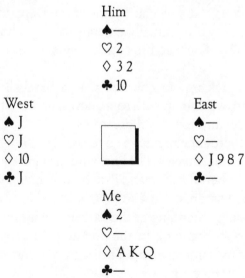

Him
♠ —
♡ 2
◊ 3 2
♣ 10

West
♠ J
♡ J
◊ 10
♣ J

East
♠ —
♡ —
◊ J 9 8 7
♣ —

Me
♠ 2
♡ —
◊ A K Q
♣ —

The sober fact of the matter is that tackling the clubs last maintains the club honors as crucial entries back to either hand.

"Paper or plastic?" the cashier asks.

· · · · · · · · ·

The supermarket *tete-a-tete* represents for me what is best about being married to your bridge partner. With only a few minor glitches—like buying birdseed instead of Rice Krispies— the shopping has been successfully completed, and we have had a lovely, meaningful bridge analysis away from the bridge table. I know for sure that if he had tried to tell me I didn't play the hand right *last night*, I would have blasted him off his chair and would have refused to talk about the hand. At least this way I got to enjoy the glow of thinking I had played the hand beautifully! And I learned a lot from the hand, also. This opportunity to delve into the intricacies of the game and come up with new nuggets of insight, while performing mundane tasks together, is a joy not shared by non-spousal partnerships.

Bridge Everywhere—Is This Wise?

After standing in the obligatory line at the Department of Motor Vehicles, we eventually emerge with a whole new structure: Jacoby Transfer Bids, including several pages of notes.

Waiting to pick up our children after a Baseball Hall of Fame field trip, we end up with some new slam investigation bids over three- and four-level preempts.

And then there's the night we go to see "The Sting" when it first opens in Los Angeles. The line winds around the block. It's thanks to Robert Redford and Paul Newman that we now play Lavinthal Discards.

The list is long. Standing at the barbecue waiting for the chicken to cook. Standing in the line at K-Mart with the mosquito nets for summer camp. The long hot summer nights without air-conditioning . . .

Is it wise—or even healthy—to talk bridge just about every place we go? Certainly in the old days it was a novelty to have one's bridge partner constantly available for refinements. Now I'm not so sure. These days we sometimes find ourselves recreating bad feelings that existed after a bad hand, and rehashing the arguments it caused. At times we seem to be unable to step back from the hand, and figure out, objectively, what went wrong.

Thus, the other day, an innocuous activity like weeding the flower beds, degenerated into a weed fight, because we couldn't agree on a bid.

This kind of stuff could turn out to be embarrassing in public places like the supermarket!

10

A Dozen Roses:
Disaster Relief

How to recover.

A DOZEN LONG-STEMMED roses, from palest pink to deepest purple red, nestling on a bed of filmy tissue paper. The card saying "Yours always."

The gangling delivery person lays these gingerly in my arms and eyes me and them with awe. "Boy, someone likes you *a lot*," he says. Yeah.

My birthday? Anniversary? Valentines Day? No. Just his attempt to apologize for going berserk at the bridge table last night.

Occasionally he suffers the slings and arrows of outrageous fortune with resigned equanimity, but not this time. The hand in question came up against two of the most obnoxious opponents in our club, the type who gloat about their top while you're still at the table, or proclaim that the contract you just went down in was cold.

I held ♠ A 3 ♡ K J 8 7 5 ◇ K 7 6 ♣ 7 5 4 and heard my partner open three spades, both vulnerable. My right-hand opponent, a sound player, bid three notrump, and that ended the auction. Being young, inexperienced and gullible, I assumed that there was a spade stopper on my right and no entry to the spades in my partner's hand. I therefore led a low heart. Not the most auspicious decision of my bridge career:

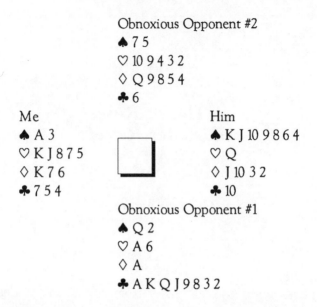

Obnoxious Opponent #2
♠ 7 5
♡ 10 9 4 3 2
◇ Q 9 8 5 4
♣ 6

Me
♠ A 3
♡ K J 8 7 5
◇ K 7 6
♣ 7 5 4

Him
♠ K J 10 9 8 6 4
♡ Q
◇ J 10 3 2
♣ 10

Obnoxious Opponent #1
♠ Q 2
♡ A 6
◇ A
♣ A K Q J 9 8 3 2

With undisguised glee, declarer won and began to run his clubs. With one club to go, this position was reached:

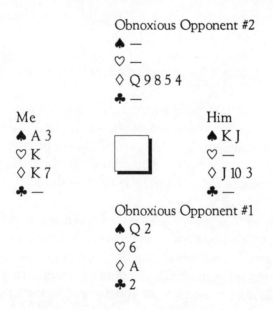

Obnoxious Opponent #2
♠ —
♡ —
◇ Q 9 8 5 4
♣ —

Me
♠ A 3
♡ K
◇ K 7
♣ —

Him
♠ K J
♡ —
◇ J 10 3
♣ —

Obnoxious Opponent #1
♠ Q 2
♡ 6
◇ A
♣ 2

By this time I was in a state of extreme misery. Partner's carding had suggested that he held the king of spades and an odd number in the suit. I also had the immediate problem of what to throw on the last club. I was so agitated by my failure to lead a spade that I failed to take the inference that if partner held another heart he would have parted with it long ago, and it was therefore "safe" for me to throw a diamond. Anyway, I made the inspired discard of the ace of spades, watching partner age a few years as I did so.

It was when the other spade in my hand hit the table that my husband lost his sanity. He and his chair lunged backward. The words that he bellowed at me, at full throttle, are irrelevant (and unprintable). Every neck in the club got whiplash as heads spun around to gape at us. Play was suspended at every table—the show at ours was riveting.

As you may well imagine, the rest of the evening, played out in icy silence, followed by the rest of the night, was not a great success.

The roses arrived the following afternoon. . . .

. . . .

There isn't a bridge player alive who doesn't face the problem of disaster recovery and crisis management, often several times in the same session. Such is the game. The excitement of living on the edge is what brings many of us back, week after week. The atmosphere of pre- and post-disasters is highly charged. Now add to this the emotional tension of being married to your partner, and the mix becomes explosive.

How do you bounce back? When you owe it to your teammates and partner to recover fast, how do you prevent one disaster from escalating into a multiple-disaster fiasco, followed by a marital crisis? Recovery is tough in any partnership, but especially hard when you're playing with Attila the Hun or your spouse. Somehow you have to delay the mental divorce proceedings and get back to the business of winning.

A bridge disaster comes in different forms. At rubber bridge it's usually an expensive three-digit number for the opponents. At matchpoints, a fat, round zero. At teams, a large IMP swing (for them). At tournaments, these are results that are unlikely to be duplicated by other sane players in the field. Recovery techniques vary somewhat, depending on the disaster.

Fixed

The easiest disaster to survive emotionally is the opponents-off-the-wall type. You and your darling spouse play every card perfectly, and they bring in an incredibly lucky slam which needs two finesses and a 2-2 split in trumps.

Recovery

Shrug your shoulders, smile at each other and make this a time of togetherness. They got lucky. Try to take comfort from the thought that in a team game it's seldom one board that decides the match.

Unlucky

Another disaster variety from which recovery is relatively easy is the measured-risk-that-doesn't-come-off type. Being a measured risk-taker is an attribute of every good bridge player. For example, you use a wonderful bidding sequence to avoid the no-spade-stopper three notrump and decide to risk the 4-3 fit in a close, vulnerable four-heart contract. This collects a double from the opponent who holds the rest of the heart suit. Minus 800 later you have to regroup and go onto the next hand.

Recovery

If you are playing in a team event, the first step on the road to recovery is to bear in mind that your opponents at the other table will be in the same boat with these hands, and may well duplicate the result. (One can always hope.) Second, this is not the time for a detailed analysis of the auction. The partner of the declarer should diffuse the tension by saying something like "Tough break" in a tone of voice that actually says "I forgive you." Bad luck and bad breaks happen in this game, and if you don't recognize that, take up Solitaire.

Asleep
The emotional terrain becomes rocky when blame can be apportioned for the disaster. The easiest type to recover from in this category is the misadventure-while-napping type. You're defending a harmless-looking one notrump and they end up making four for a score of 180. It's only when you wake up to peer at the score sheet, and notice that you have an unmistakable bottom, that the realization dawns a disaster has occurred.

Recovery
Recovery is relatively simple, since this disaster carries with it no prior emotional baggage. Do not cause problems by attempting a discussion of the defense in the one minute before the next hand. Such snap analyses are usually wrong anyway, so the net effect is going to be a bad feeling in the partnership, which will sow the seeds for disaster on the next hand. Concentrate your energies (such as they are) on waking up.

Paralysed
The most difficult type of disaster to recover from, especially for spouses, is the obvious cataclysmic catastrophe that becomes apparent early in the hand and causes one's body to go paralysed from shock.

- Your partner has bid seven hearts off a cashable ace and they've just led and cashed that ace.

- You've been passed in a cuebid and are playing in a 2-1 fit at the five-level. Vulnerable.

- You've just seen that your discard will enable them to make an otherwise unmakable vulnerable game.

• One look at dummy has told you that their five spades doubled and redoubled contract is cold.

Recovery

How do you recover? The hand is over; the opponents are bouncing all over their chairs and you and your spouse want to kill each other.

In our calm and rational moments, I am sure that we all recognize the need for speedy recovery. Coming back at the table, however, in the midst of murderous passion, is more easily said than done. Every molecule wants to scream out, accuse, and justify. Even though you know that a flaming argument at this point can only decrease your concentration further and increase your opponents' delight and sense of victory.

But come back you must if you are to have any hope of salvaging the match or the session. Against all bodily intuition you must be cool and outwardly impassive. Before starting the next hand, you must take your time. Take, also, some long, slow deep breaths, and use whatever techniques you normally use to zero in at the start of a session. This will require a deliberate, conscious effort. Don't let the opponents rush you as they gallop along with their momentum.

The key to recovery is strict and unconditional enforcement of the no-discussion-following-a-hand rule. If you are disciplined in this, but your partner persists in jabbering on at you, do not respond. Tune him out! And don't get sucked into discussion either with the line "This may come up again this match. . . ."

He's lying. It won't. Your main job is to regain your concentration.

Those two minutes following a major disaster are the most emotionally charged in a marital partnership. Light a match at that table and the whole room will explode. If you can survive those two minutes and bring yourself back, you will find that the passion dissipates surprisingly quickly, especially if you can achieve a good result on the next board.

I remember a description of the 1985 Bermuda Bowl, with its cliff-hanger semifinal match between Brazil and the USA. The match was close all the way. On the final day, San Francisco's Hugh Ross and the late Peter Pender had disasters on three consecutive boards. The first one was mundane— they played in the wrong game and lost 11 IMPs. The following two boards were the wrenching, sinking-heart type of disasters, in which they were doubled and went for 800 both times! Those three deals cost the USA 37 IMPs.

"Could [they] react calmly and efficiently in the face of such disasters?" Henry Francis wrote in his BULLETIN report. "Lesser mortals might have lost their composure and engaged in all kinds of antics to try to get back the lost IMPs. Not Ross and Pender."

On the *very next board* Ross and Pender defended a close three notrump with cool and deadly precision, sinking the contract by one trick, and gaining 5 IMPs for the USA instead of losing 10 IMPs to Brazil. The United States won the match by just 9 IMPs, and then went on to win the Bermuda Bowl.

I remember marvelling at the fact that Ross and Pender could pull off such a feat of perfect timing and concentration *in the midst of total catastrophe*. This marked them forever in my mind as truly great champions.

· · · · · · · · ·

Postmortem

The dozen roses incident, which occurred many years ago, brought with it two major lessons for me and my partner. First, I should have led the ace of spades. Not because it worked on the given hand, but because it won in the postmortem! By not leading my partner's suit, I poisoned the atmosphere psychologically, setting us up for a massive explosion if my alternative lead didn't work. Not one iota of sympathy did I get from my bridge friends when I wept on their shoulders with this hand.

Partner *did* open three spades, vulnerable. The lesson I learned was this:

- Make bids and plays that win in the postmortem. In the long run this improves both bridge results and marital harmony.

Second, while it was gratifying to know that my husband still loved me, despite my opening lead, the roses were a band-aid solution for a major wound. Disasters are part of this crazy game of bridge, even at the highest levels, and if we can't weather them in a sane and civilized manner, at the table, we might as well not play.

11

Bridge Orphans:
The Children

♡♡ ♡ ♡

HOW TO SHIELD THEM FROM THE SORDIDNESS.
HOW TO LIVE WITH THE GUILT.

MY YOUNGER DAUGHTER, six years old, is watching me pack
for a bridge weekend.

"When *I* grow up and have children," she says to me, "*I*
won't leave them to go play bridge."

I pause.

"Well, darling, that will be your choice," I say to her.
"Mommy also had a choice. Whether to play bridge, or
whether to play bridge and have children." She is quiet for a
long while, digesting this.

I am not as nasty as I sound. I never find it easy to tell my
girls that we're leaving for a weekend. Even though they love

the baby-sitters, who will spoil them rotten while we're away, they sure know how to push those guilt buttons.

. . . .

About a year later, when my older daughter is nine, we are playing in the District Finals of the Grand National Pairs. The top three pairs in our district will win a free trip to the nationals, and because this year it's in Hawaii, everyone is especially motivated.

We are flowing. We have qualified comfortably for the second day and are lying fifth overall after the first session of the second day. Now we are two-thirds of the way through the evening session, and are having a magical time. Every close slam and game that we're bidding is coming home; every contract that we're doubling is going for numbers; and everyone who is doubling us is regretting it. Even my chronic overbidding is paying off, for once! I am beginning to smell the ocean and plan my Hawaiian wardrobe.

The Phone Call

My husband has just executed a lovely double squeeze to bring home a close six-notrump contract, when the Director comes to our table and tells us that we're wanted on the phone and that we should go swiftly because it sounds urgent.

Only people with children can know the terror of such a message. We race to the nearest phone and I grip the receiver with icy hands. I hear my baby-sitter apologizing for disturbing us. She tells me that the girls were playing airplane in the family room (!) and my elder daughter fell on her head on the stone fireplace. There's no visible wound, but the child is screaming so hysterically, that she (the sitter) is alarmed, and wonders if she should take her to the hospital.

"No," I say. "Call the pediatrician and follow her advice. We'll call back in 15 minutes."

Our hearts are in our mouths as we rush back to the playing area, in time for the next round. Our concentration is shot, but, miraculously, the Guardian Angel of Bridge continues to watch over us. On the first hand, our opponents reach a hopelessly wrong contract, and as long as we just follow suit we will get a top board. On the second hand, they fail to locate the queen of trumps in a two-way guess situation, so we will do well on this board, too.

After the round we charge back to the phone and call home. "Good news," my baby-sitter says. "The pediatrician says that it's an excellent sign that she's screaming so much. It's supposedly a bad sign if they get drowsy after the fall. So, we're just to watch her and calm her down. If there's still a problem tomorrow, you can bring her in."

There's no question that we're calmed by the news. However, the sound of my child's heart-rending screams in the background do not exactly reassure me. It seems that when the baby-sitter mentioned that she may have to go to the hospital, my daughter reached new levels of screaming power.

"Can you put her on the phone?" I ask the sitter. Apparently, this is not possible. My older daughter, too, knows how to push the buttons.

"We'll call back later," I say, and we run back for the next round. This is the round in which our opponents bid a close slam and go down on a brutal trump break. Then, on the second board, they make a lead-directing double that enables *us* to bid a close slam, because now I know which ace my partner has. This 24-point slam just rolls, and I feel sure that we have two tops.

One more round is left in this strange evening and it is uneventful. During the scoring, we return to the phone and are assured that everything seems to be OK. My daughter has calmed down and is drinking apple juice. She still won't come to the phone, however.

Three pairs in the field, including us, have had huge games, and we end up third overall. To our joy, this wins us the free trip to Hawaii. I find it hard to describe my feelings at the time: All intermingled are the terror of my daughter's fall, the guilt of not being there, the joy of having a perfect bridge session, and the thrill of winning this marvellous trip.

The Guilt

So there you have it, in all its soap-opera glory: the drama, the heartache, the ambivalence. Like the proverbial oil and water, children and serious bridge don't mix. Tournament bridge is not exactly a wholesome family activity; and as the parents of two adorable children, our lives are filled with dilemmas and contradictions.

I ask myself, why is it that even though we love our kids, we abandon them to play in bridge tournaments? That every time we leave the house for a bridge trip and see those faces with the big eyes watching at the window, I feel like the witch in Hansel and Gretel? The Devil Bridge Player in me replies that the answer is simple: Tournament bridge is one of the things you love doing most in the world. Leaving your children for the occasional weekend helps teach them independence. Look, It's *good* for the kids to learn at an early age that they're not the beginning and end of your universe, merely the brightest constellations in it.

Why is it that even though we hire baby-sitters who treat the children better than we do, we still feel guilty? That even though the sitters are bright, athletic people who expand our daughters' horizons in ways that are beyond us—by taking them sailing and skiing for example—we somehow feel that we are short-changing the kids? That no matter how much money we pay the sitters, we feel that it is not enough?

The Devil is glib with the answer: the quality of the baby-sitters is irrelevant. Mothers are programmed to feel guilty when they leave their kids, or select activities that do not include their kids. Don't feel bad. You want your children to see that all things are possible for them—families, careers and recreation. You believe that you provide this role model for them.

Why do we feel the need to buy them gorgeous presents when we're away for more than two days? Is it because we never completely escape when we're away and they're on our minds? Is it to compensate them for our absence and assuage our guilt? Is it because we need them to have *some* positive feelings associated with our going away? No, says the Devil Bridge Player, you're reading too much into it. What better way to spend the long morning hours before the first session than shopping for the children!

Why is it that the night our daughter fell on her head, I felt that we were being punished? Don't be silly, says my friend the Devil. Children take tumbles all the time. It's no big deal that it happened one time when you weren't home.

· · · · · · · · ·

And so my bridge life swirls about my children, like radioactive dust.

· · · · · · · · ·

The phone rings and my younger daughter answers it.

"Hullo," says the voice. "Call to the phone the lady of the house or anyone who plays bridge."

As I have trained her to do, my baby says, "My mother can't come to the phone right now. Can I take a message?"

"Sure," says the voice. "Tell her she holds the ace, king, ex, ex, ex of spades, jack ex of hearts. . . ."

Later, when I get home, I ask, "Any messages?"

"Yeah, one of your crazy bridge friends," my daughter says. (She already has us figured out.)

"Which one?" I ask.

"Oh, he says you'll recognize the hand," she sniffs, handing me the sheet of hieroglyphics. She tosses her head and rolls her eyes. All *her* friends are *normal*.

Another time my older daughter answers the phone and a voice rasps at her in a loud whisper, "Don't be afraid. Get your mother."

"Uh, sure," my child says, and breezily runs to call me. "Mom, you have an obscene phone call on the upstairs phone."

Puzzled, I go to take the call and find that it's another of my "crazy bridge friends," who, despite *acute laryngitis*, has called to discuss last night's bridge hands!

The Sordid Underbelly

While the aspect of Leaving the Children fills me with guilt, there's another side of bridge that I feel the urge to protect them from. The thought of exposing them to the Bridge Scene, the sordid underbelly of my life, makes me cringe. At the same time that I confess some of my best friends are bridge players, part of me winces as I observe the tournament scene through my children's eyes.

"Mom, why are those people yelling so much? Are they deaf?"

"Why are people smoking in the bathrooms even though the sign says *No Smoking*? Are they blind?"

"Look at all this garbage lying around!"

"Why are these people such bad sports?"

And later, at the restaurant:

"Boy! Listen to the people at that table yelling about bridge. With their mouths full! They're making so much noise that everyone in the restaurant is looking at them and they don't even know it!"

We tournament bridge players are so saturated with bridge that we become bad-mannered, loud-mouthed slobs. Are these the adults that I want my children to emulate?

"Boy! Are *these* the people you're with when you go away?"

How can I explain that *we are* these people, and that bridge brings out the worst in us, too? They know it causes tension between us, even though we supposedly don't talk bridge in front of them. We try hard to shield them from this seamy side of our lives, not always successfully. . . .

It is a Friday night and we are on the very last hand at the local duplicate game. With no opposing bidding, I have just become the declarer at four hearts. The queen-of-spades opening lead is on the table.

Him
♠ A K 7 2
♡ J 9 5 4
♢ Q J 7 6 5
♣ —

□

Me
♠ 4
♡ A 7 6 2
♢ A 8 4
♣ K J 10 8 4

West	Him	East	Me
—	1 ♢	Pass	2 ♣
Pass	2 ♢	Pass	2 ♡
Pass	3 ♡	Pass	4 ♡
Pass	Pass	Pass	

The post-bidding discussion reveals that earlier my partner had a heart in with his diamonds—it's way past bed-time after all—and therefore fate has decreed that *I* should be declarer on this hand.

The play looks dicey, but after much cogitating, I think I see a possible route to ten tricks, but it will require some luck. My plan is to take two top spades, two trumps (the ace and a small one, after trumps have been drawn), two spade ruffs in my hand and four diamonds. The dummy entries and general control problems seem to elude me for the moment, but I forge ahead.

I win the spade and immediately ruff a spade. If they're giving honest count, it looks as if the spades are 4-4. Good! Now a heart to the nine produces the queen from East. Back comes a low club, ten, queen, and I have to ruff. I ruff a second spade in hand and cash the ace of hearts, everyone following. Only the king of hearts is out. Here is the position:

Dummy
♠ K
♡ J
◊ Q J 7 6 5
♣ —

□

Me
♠ —
♡ —
◊ A 8 4
♣ K J 8 4

At this stage I have lost only one trick. I have five in the bag, and need five more. According to my "plan," they are supposed to be the king of spades and four diamond tricks.

I start praying that the diamonds divide 3-2 and that the person with the king of diamonds does not also have the king of hearts. I play ace of diamonds and a diamond. My right-hand opponent wins and I hold my breath. But the gods are not with me tonight. East unerringly draws the last heart and plays a club to his partner's ace. Down one.

If East had *not* held the king of hearts, and had returned a club, I'm not sure I would have made this hand, anyway. Although dummy was now high (except for the trump), my hand still had club losers. I suppose I would have to put in the eight of clubs and hope it forced the ace.

We open the score slip. I shrug my shoulders. We have a dreadful score for going down one in four hearts. Three pairs are in four, making, and the rest of the pairs are in three hearts making either three or four. Only one other pair shares my misery in four down one.

Now my husband says my favorite four words when I've just gone down in a tough contract: "The hand is cold."

"Thanks a lot," I tell him. "Why not let my misery settle a little, before giving me the benefit of your analysis?"

In the Kitchen

We drive home in silence, and pay the baby-sitter. The hand is stuck in my head and I can't think of a better line of play. "How is it cold?" I say, eventually. We are downstairs in the kitchen and write out the whole hand on a napkin:

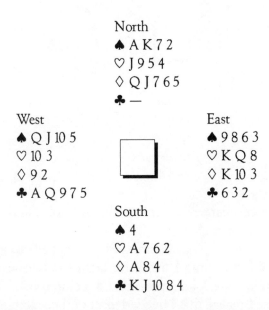

```
                    North
                    ♠ A K 7 2
                    ♡ J 9 5 4
                    ◇ Q J 7 6 5
                    ♣ —
West                                East
♠ Q J 10 5                          ♠ 9 8 6 3
♡ 10 3                              ♡ K Q 8
◇ 9 2                               ◇ K 10 3
♣ A Q 9 7 5                         ♣ 6 3 2
                    South
                    ♠ 4
                    ♡ A 7 6 2
                    ◇ A 8 4
                    ♣ K J 10 8 4
```

Here's the line of play that he suggests: (looking at all four hands, of course.) "To me this looks like a simple cross-ruff. Win the spade, and immediately play the queen of diamonds. Let's assume that East doesn't cover, his best play. Finesse, then come to hand with the ace of diamonds, and lead the king of clubs, planning to ruff it in dummy. When West covers, ruff in dummy, cash the king of spades, pitching a diamond, then ruff a spade in your hand.

"Now play the jack of clubs, ruffing West's queen, and ruff the last spade. You can now cash the good ten of clubs. By this time you have brought in nine tricks. Here's the position:" (Scribble, scribble.)

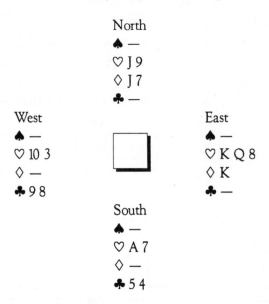

North
♠ —
♡ J 9
◊ J 7
♣ —

West
♠ —
♡ 10 3
◊ —
♣ 9 8

East
♠ —
♡ K Q 8
◊ K
♣ —

South
♠ —
♡ A 7
◊ —
♣ 5 4

"The ace of hearts is a sure tenth, and you might even maneuver an overtrick."

"It's a nice line of play," I admit, "But it's not as *cold* as you make out. On your line I need the diamond finesse, a 3-2 diamond split, a 4-4 spade split and a 5-3 club split."

Of course I realize that I needed most of those things (and more) with the line-of-play I actually took, but his suggestion that I can make an overtrick is going too far. "With this distribution, I see no way to maneuver your so-called overtrick!"

He frowns at the napkin. I'm still feeling sensitive about going down in this game, and am extremely irritated by his snap criticisms at the table.

"Perhaps there is no overtrick," he concedes.

"What do you mean, *perhaps*," I dig in. "Look at the hands. There's no way to make an overtrick in this end position."

The hand is interesting and we've both warmed up. The best line of play is clearly the cross-ruff—my line was just too complicated, setting up side suits, cross-ruffing and drawing trumps all at the same time. I would concede that his line is better, but I just don't like the condescending way he has of explaining it. We're talking quite loudly now.

Always Cashing Aces

"Look, what I don't like about the way *you* played the hand," he says to me, "is that by cashing the ace of diamonds you gave up control of the hand. Somewhere in a beginner book you once read that with the ace opposite a queen-jack combination, you should play the ace and then low towards the queen. I notice that you're always cashing aces." I am stung.

"I don't understand why every time we discuss a hand that *you* didn't make," I say, angrily, "we agree that you took a view that didn't work and that's the end of it. When *I* go down, however, the discussion always veers toward some generalization about an inherent weakness in my game." I'm up from the table and stomping around the kitchen. "*You're always cashing aces*," I mimic in a falsetto voice. "Boy! Your arrogance just kills me."

He tells me that he thinks I'm being ridiculous, and before long we're shouting at each other, and the whole thing has gotten out of hand.

A little flurry of white comes hurtling into the kitchen, my younger daughter, all crumpled from sleep and red in the face. "Stop it!" she screams at us. "Stop! Stop! Stop!"

She runs up to me and punches me on the arm with her fists clenched. "Stop yelling at Daddy!" Then she runs up to him and starts pummeling him for all she's worth. "I hate bridge!" she cries. "It's a dumb game!"

We comfort her, and soothe her, and stroke her head, and tell her that she's right, it's just a stupid game, that we just got a little too excited about a hand, and that we weren't *really* fighting (a lie). We then take her up to bed and tuck her in. Before rolling over and going back to sleep, she says to me "You shouldn't play bridge. Nice people don't talk like that."

The Guilt Revisited

The kitchen scene is the Sordid Underbelly at its worst. We are chastened. We had always imagined that late at night, after the game, the kids were deep in slumber, far, far away from our nocturnal "discussions."

Ever since that scene, we have restricted our arguments to the drive home, or, after a really bad session, we simply don't talk to each other, which tends to mask the friction from the kids. Now that they're older, however, they've became more discerning, and can usually tell when there are bad bridge vibes in the house.

Bridge and Children—How to Manage Both

- Acknowledge that having children does not mean giving up activities that you enjoyed *before* the children. Obviously you'll have to modify your life, but having children should not be synonymous with changing your identity.

- Do not take the children with you to tournaments. Spare them! Bridge is an adults' world.*

- Planning is the key. Spend hours beforehand cultivating wonderful baby-sitters who will ease the angst when you leave for a weekend.

- Recognize that wonderful sitters are worth their weight in gold. Find out what the going rate is and then pay them much more. This will make them want to come back.

- Treat your children with the same courtesy you reserve for other non-bridge players: don't discuss bridge in front of them.

- Try to resolve conflicts in a way that shields your kids from bridge arguments. If you don't, they will find it hard to understand why you go away to play a game that causes so much discord.

---

* until such time, at least, when Junior Bridge tournaments become a popular social activity.

12

Couple's Caper:
Romantic Bridge Weekend

♡♡

IS A ROMANTIC BRIDGE WEEKEND
A CONTRADICTION IN TERMS?

THIS IS A chapter about conjugal romance at bridge tournaments: a short chapter. Unless you get married at the bridge
tournament, I'm not sure that there is such a thing as a
romantic bridge weekend with your spouse. As we wend our
way through a bridge weekend, I fantasize how things might
be different, if this were a romantic golf weekend.

The Planning

*Imagine a romantic golf weekend, in the Poconos, say. I write
away for brochures and spend hours watching my husband drool
over glossy pictures of lush, rolling golf courses. Then there are the
rooms! Circular beds with black velvet covers. Mirrors on the
ceilings. A private swimming pool (in the room!). A heart-shaped
jacuzzi. The brochure shows a gorgeous woman, the type you don't
encounter in real life, reclining in the jacuzzi, with bubbles up to her
neck. A long, slender arm holds a long slender glass of pink
champagne.*

*It takes quite a while to select what we want, but eventually we
mail our reservation request in a plain brown paper envelope.*

♡ ♡ ♡ ♡ ♡ ♡ ♡ ♡ ♡

Planning for the romantic bridge weekend happens by
accident. I call the hotel and ask them about their special
weekend rates.

"Well, if you want a *romantic* weekend," the desk clerk says
to me, "you can get our Couple's Caper for $49.00. This
includes a room with a king-size bed, champagne on ice, a box
of chocolates and breakfast the next morning."

"Is there a special rate for the bridge tournament?" I ask.

"Oh yes," she replies. "$47.00 for a double room."

"Fine. I'll take the Couple's Caper," I say.

"Oh no, you can't do that," she says to me. "If you're with the
bridge group you have to take the bridge rate."

"Let me check with my bridge partner and call you back,"
I reply.

This conversation took place on a Monday morning. On
Wednesday afternoon I call again and, since I didn't give my
name the first time, I reserve for us the Couple's Caper.

"So now it's a romantic weekend," he says to me.

The Arrival

*As the car meanders along the woodsy roads and approaches
the resort in its idyllic surroundings, we see that we have truly
escaped from life's travails. We check into our glitzy room. Wow!
The glossy ads didn't lie. It's a glorious day, and, hand in hand, we
explore this strange haven, checking out the place. We visit the Pro
shop to arrange starting times, and I watch him inhaling the heady
aroma of pine and golf-carts. As I hug him, I feel his every molecule
quivering.*

♡ ♡ ♡ ♡ ♡ ♡ ♡ ♡ ♡

For our romantic bridge weekend, we arrive in the city and
get stuck in traffic because of construction on the highway.

We hold hands in the car and discuss our conventions. Eventually we're installed in the hotel, and, sure enough, there are chocolates and champagne on the king-size bed. If sex is going to happen at all this weekend, the best time is now, right after check-in, just before the first session.

The Afternoon

Nine glorious holes of golf, each hole a stunning revelation of trees, ponds and emerald greens. Dappled sunlight and gentle breezes. Golf, like bridge, is a daunting experience, but the frustrations we feel are not with each other. We are great friends on the golf course, and loudly applaud all good shots. Romantically, we set off into the woods together to hunt for lost balls.

♡ ♡ ♡ ♡ ♡ ♡ ♡ ♡ ♡

Twenty-six glorious hands of bridge, each deal a challenge of wits. We plunge in, with tension and expectations high. Matchpoints is a killer game—every lapse in concentration draws blood. So it's not long before we are at odds with one another, going through the usual rigmarole of parry, thrust, wound and kill. The only romance in this encounter is in the ancient fantasy sense of Saint George slaying the dragon!

The Dinner Hour

Golf is over. Back to our hotel room to enjoy its amenities. The logistics of us plus champagne in the jacuzzi are more easily imagined than done, but eventually, there we are, bubbles everywhere.

Afterwards, I drape myself in the filmy, diaphanous outfit that I wouldn't be seen dead in at home, and we take a leisurely twilight stroll to the candlelit restaurant in the pines. Again, everything that was advertised is here: soft music, romantic atmosphere, dreamy food and luscious desserts. We clink our wine glasses and think that we want to stay married forever. A photographer records this moment and sells it to us in a heart-shaped frame.

♡ ♡ ♡ ♡ ♡ ♡ ♡ ♡ ♡

The bridge session is finally over, and despite the intense dislike I feel for my husband at this point in time, I decide to go along with him and the usual gang for dinner. Dinner consists of a quick bite and loud comparison of scores at a nearby, crowded restaurant. We opt for light fare, as we want *some* blood left in our heads for the evening session. No wine either, since we have a hard enough time playing the right cards *without* alcohol. As we rehash this awful game, I think that at this moment I could happily divorce him.

Night-time

A cabaret show at the resort, followed by dancing to the strains of an old-fashioned band. Then back in our room we snuggle up on the circular bed to watch a late-night movie.

♡ ♡ ♡ ♡ ♡ ♡ ♡ ♡ ♡

Back at the romantic bridge weekend:

North-South vulnerable

```
                        North
                        ♠ 4 3
                        ♡ 7 4
                        ◇ J 10 9 6 4 2
                        ♣ A 10 7
        West (Me)
        ♠ K 2
        ♡ K 9 2              [         ]
        ◇ Q 7               [         ]
        ♣ K Q 8 6 5 2
```

West	North	East	South
1 ♣	Pass	1 ♡	1 ♠
2 ♡	Pass	Pass	2 ♠
3 ♣	3 ♠	Double	Pass
Pass	Pass		

   I am West, on lead with this collection of aceless wonders, and, as has been the case most of the day, I do not have a good feeling about this hand. Eventually, I select the two of hearts, and partner's ten produces the queen from declarer, who has visibly brightened. He now cashes the ace of hearts and ruffs a heart. Then comes a spade finesse, and again I'm on lead.

   This time I play the king of clubs, taken on the board, and now declarer plays the jack of diamonds. East plays low very smoothly, but this declarer is on the ball. My partner, the intrepid doubler, has not shown up with anything higher than a jack so far. Thus, declarer confidently plays the king. The hand is over. South concedes a diamond and has made four. Recall, he was in three, doubled. These were the hands:

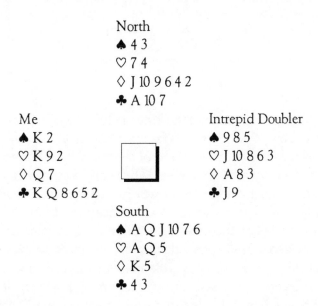

North
♠ 4 3
♡ 7 4
◇ J 10 9 6 4 2
♣ A 10 7

Me
♠ K 2
♡ K 9 2
◇ Q 7
♣ K Q 8 6 5 2

Intrepid Doubler
♠ 9 8 5
♡ J 10 8 6 3
◇ A 8 3
♣ J 9

South
♠ A Q J 10 7 6
♡ A Q 5
◇ K 5
♣ 4 3

   "Why do you *torture* me with these doubles?" I hiss at him. "Why must I age ten years every time we play matchpoints?"

   "Why do you destroy me with (a) your stupid bidding, and (b) your crummy defense?" he shoots back at me. "Your three-club bid is a gross overbid, and then you followed it up with the most asinine opening lead I ever saw in my life!"

   "One of these days, just *one* of these days," I say bitterly, "you are going to hold as much as a *queen* in your suit, and the earth is going to move."

North
♠ 4 3
♡ 7 4
◊ J 10 9 6 4 2
♣ A 10 7

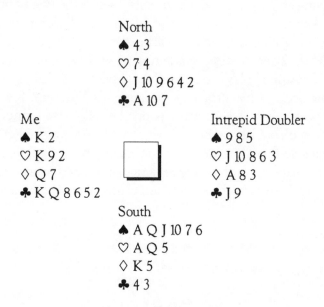

Me
♠ K 2
♡ K 9 2
◊ Q 7
♣ K Q 8 6 5 2

Intrepid Doubler
♠ 9 8 5
♡ J 10 8 6 3
◊ A 8 3
♣ J 9

South
♠ A Q J 10 7 6
♡ A Q 5
◊ K 5
♣ 4 3

"Look, if you just lead the king of clubs like a human being at trick one, this contract is far from iron-clad," he continues. "Declarer wins either the first or second club in dummy and must now try a heart finesse. When this loses, you can now return a third club, which I will ruff to prevent a diamond pitch. Now declarer will play ace of hearts and ruff his losing heart, and is at the crossroads. Should he use this entry to finesse a spade or to play a diamond? If he finesses a spade, he's dead. He must now lose two diamonds, and will be down one."

"All very pat," I say, "but you're wrong. For your double, you're much more likely to have the ace of diamonds than the badly placed king of spades. He's almost sure to use that entry for the diamond play. Then he'll make three doubled, rather than four doubled, and we will merely have a bottom, rather than a double bottom. So, to repeat my earlier question, *Why do you torture me with these doubles?*"

And so on. Back and forth. Round and round. Bile rising. Frustration eating us like acid. Not foreplay.

Bedtime

A splash in the private pool. Another romp in the jacuzzi. A Very Romantic Interlude.

♡ ♡ ♡ ♡ ♡ ♡ ♡ ♡ ♡

We return to our room, and from aggravation, I eat half the box of chocolates. I praise the heavens for the Couple's Caper king-size bed. This way, he can climb in on his side, I can climb in on my side, and it's like we're in different countries, which suits me fine.

The Final Analysis

If you want a romantic weekend *with your spouse*, don't make it a bridge weekend. Golf. Skiing. Sight-seeing. *Anything* but bridge! If it must be bridge, then let the bridge happen with a different partner.

13

Between Sessions: Postmortems and Indigestion

"LET'S GO CHINESE," I offer.

"Let's not," he counters. "I'd really rather have something American, like a hamburger."

It figures. This is how our bidding has gone all afternoon, so why should dinner be different? We end up in a small, smoky Italian restaurant with the usual crazy gang.

The Cast of Characters

Sitting across from me is the Lunatic, our friend who enjoys his status of being certifiably insane. The actions that he takes at the bridge table guarantee him this title for life. Also, the way he goes nuts at his partners makes my husband seem like Mary Poppins.

Then there's our friend, the Expert, who is always giving

unsolicited advice and sometimes analyzes hands based on hindsight. You cannot tell him anything about bridge. He knows it all.

Sitting on the right is the Bandit, who has earned this title with his unnerving table presence. He steals shamelessly from his opponents at the bridge table.

Across from me is the Mona Lisa, the Bandit's partner in today's event. She is in the unenviable position of being new to tournament bridge, and is therefore perceived by the crowd as weak when she gets a poor score and lucky when she does well. She's actually a respectable bridge player, who listens to all our baloney with an enigmatic smile, hence the nickname. She doesn't waste her time justifying her plays.

On my left is the Whiner, the unluckiest player in the world. He always plays perfectly and is constantly being fixed by people like the Mona Lisa.

Finally, there's the Judge, an anomaly in this group: quietly spoken, and an outstanding bridge player. He's the one person here whose opinions I really trust.

The Postmortems

The afternoon Open Pairs session was pretty grim for me and my partner. Usually you play an entire session of bridge in one direction, North-South or East-West. Today, however, we played a Howell Movement, in which the pairs switch directions after every round. This should have no effect on one's bridge game, but for some reason it seemed like wherever we sat there was a terrible bridge problem. Every auction was like a tug-of-war and every defense a contest. Even on the play of the hands we failed to see eye to eye on what was right. Despite my best intentions, we started to argue midway through the afternoon, and now, at dinner time, I feel miserable. I have no appetite for food or rehashed hands.

We untangle the hand records from our convention cards, napkins and menus, and, like pagans performing some strange ritual, we start at Board 1, comparing our scores and sharing our triumphs and tragedies.

We're on Board 7, when the waitress approaches our table and asks if we're ready to order. It's apparent that no one has opened a menu yet, and the waitress backs away nervously. She's never seen—or heard—a group quite like this one. After cursory glances at the menu and some quick decisions, we resume our perusal of Board 7:

South dealer
Both sides vulnerable

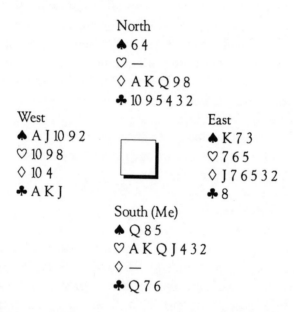

North
♠ 6 4
♡ —
◊ A K Q 9 8
♣ 10 9 5 4 3 2

West
♠ A J 10 9 2
♡ 10 9 8
◊ 10 4
♣ A K J

East
♠ K 7 3
♡ 7 6 5
◊ J 7 6 5 3 2
♣ 8

South (Me)
♠ Q 8 5
♡ A K Q J 4 3 2
◊ —
♣ Q 7 6

I share our ill-fated auction when I held the South cards.

Me	West	Him	East
1 ♡	1 ♠	Double	2 ♠
3 ♡	Pass	3 ♠	Pass
4 ♡	Double	Pass	Pass
Pass			

My partner's double was negative, showing the minors. His three-spade bid commanded me to bid a minor. When I didn't, he got his characteristic, exasperated look, and when we got doubled, he started sighing like a windstorm.

I grimace. "They led the ace of clubs, and it was bye-bye. Down three—minus 800."

"Why are you such a feminist?" the Expert teases me. "When the man says bid a minor, bid a minor! You got what you deserved."

"Perhaps you should have passed three hearts," the Judge advises my husband. "This hand has *misfit* written all over it."

"I *opened* four hearts in first seat," the Expert announces, pretty pleased with himself, "so I got to play the hand undoubled."

"Never mind," the Lunatic says to me, "I saved you from a complete bottom. I opened the hand *five* hearts." A momentary hush falls over the table. Even for the Lunatic, this is over the top. By way of explanation, he tells us that he was playing against the Bandit. Everyone always fears that the Bandit will rob them blind, and does crazy things against him. The Mona Lisa smiles. She's the one who got to double five hearts.

The Whiner, who was sitting East on the hand, heard his partner open one spade out of turn. North did not accept, and South, somewhat nervous now, opened *three* hearts. West, sticking to his guns, overcalled three spades. "Now listen to this," the Whiner complains. "North doubled. For *penalties*. The only pair in the room playing penalty doubles in that auction! So we went down one for an absolute bottom."

The dinner finally arrives, and there's quite a flurry of papers and plates as we rearrange our cards and hand records while trying to fit the food on the table. The waitress can't figure out where to put the side orders of spaghetti, and eventually just gives them to people in their hands. With spaghetti held aloft, we go on to discuss Board 19.

My stomach contracts as I look at this hand again. Miserably, I pick at my food. I deserve the Dumb Prize for my defense here.

South dealer
East-West vulnerable

North
♠ 6 4 3 2
♡ A 9 5 3
◇ K 2
♣ A 4 2

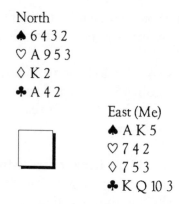

East (Me)
♠ A K 5
♡ 7 4 2
◇ 7 5 3
♣ K Q 10 3

At unfavorable vulnerability for us, the bidding had gone:

South	Him	North	Me
1 ◇	2 ♡	Double	3 ♡
4 ♠	Pass	Pass	Pass

My partner led the two of hearts, and declarer played the ace, pitching a diamond from his hand. Now a low spade came off the board, and I won the king. I was truly baffled. Why would partner lead the *two* of hearts when he had K-Q-J-10? Obviously he wanted a ruff, but in what suit? My clubs were longer than my diamonds, so I played the king of clubs. Declarer won this on the board, and partner didn't ruff. My partner seemed to be very unhappy—what else is new?—and when declarer played another spade off the board, I absent-mindedly played the ace, dropping my partner's queen! Declarer now made five! Partner had an apoplectic fit!

Here were the hands:

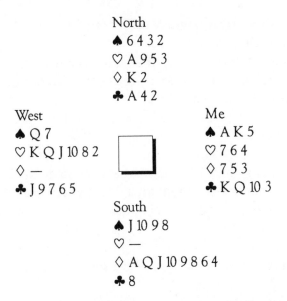

North
♠ 6 4 3 2
♡ A 9 5 3
◇ K 2
♣ A 4 2

West
♠ Q 7
♡ K Q J 10 8 2
◇ —
♣ J 9 7 6 5

Me
♠ A K 5
♡ 7 6 4
◇ 7 5 3
♣ K Q 10 3

South
♠ J 10 9 8
♡ —
◇ A Q J 10 9 8 6 4
♣ 8

"That doubleton diamond on the board, and my own balanced hand, created a total mental block for me," I tell my friends. "I simply could not visualize an eight-card suit in declarer's hand!"

"You didn't *think*," my husband blasts me. (A Maalox moment—the spaghetti isn't sitting well.) "In order for me to be void in clubs, declarer would have to have *six* of them. Not exactly possible once she opened one diamond and then rebid four spades! The suit I wanted *had* to be diamonds. It's not hard. It's all logical. Then that dumb play of the ace of spades. Ugh!" He shudders, viciously stabbing his spaghetti. I'm relieved it's not me on that plate.

There's a moment of silence as people digest my defense. Everyone agrees with him that I was truly dumb.

"The hand is cold if declarer plays the nine of hearts at trick one!" the Expert offers.

The Mona Lisa, who would never dream of underleading K-Q-J-10 of hearts, led the king against four spades. Then, whenever she or the Bandit got in with spades, they kept leading hearts. Declarer lost control of the hand.

The Judge's partner opened three diamonds with the

South hand, and the Judge bid three notrump. Plus 630 earned them a bundle of matchpoints.

"I opened *five* diamonds," the Lunatic contributes.

"We doubled them in four hearts," the Whiner chips in, "and, my luck, they made five."

"Why would you ever let them play in four hearts?" the Expert asks him.

"Dessert anyone?" The waitress has been standing there for awhile, waiting for us to notice her. My stomach heaves at the thought of something rich going into it, but everyone else is gung-ho.

The last board we discuss, Board 26, is a beauty.

East dealer
Both sides vulnerable

```
                        North
                        ♠ K 5 4 2
                        ♡ Q 9 6 4 2
                        ◇ 3
                        ♣ A K 3
        West                            East
        ♠ Q J 10 6                      ♠ 9 3
        ♡ 10 8 5                        ♡ K J 7
        ◇ K Q 7                         ◇ 10 9 8 6
        ♣ 10 6 4                        ♣ J 9 7 5
                        South
                        ♠ A 8 7
                        ♡ A 3
                        ◇ A J 5 4 2
                        ♣ Q 8 2
```

There was no opposing bidding, and we ended up in three notrump, with my husband, the declarer, holding the South hand. The queen of spades was led, and it went duck, duck,

duck. A spade was continued, won by the ace in declarer's hand. Now my partner played ace of hearts and a heart, won in the East hand by the jack.

East shifted to the ten of diamonds, which sent my partner into the tank for five minutes. He eventually played the ace of diamonds, went to dummy with a club, and played a heart, clearing the heart suit. East, in with the king of hearts, played another diamond, and that sounded the death knell for this contract. Partner lost two diamonds, two hearts, and a spade.

Interestingly, the postmortem reveals that both the Expert and the Lunatic played the hand the same way, with the same sad result.

"Isn't there a general principle here?" I say. "If you can't afford a switch to a new suit, then you can't afford to duck? Clearly, you guys all made the wrong play at trick one when you ducked the spade. Suppose you play the hand in exactly the same way, but instead of ducking the first spade, you win with the ace in your hand. Now if there's any kind of reasonable situation in diamonds, all you'll lose is two diamonds and two hearts. No spade loser."

They all start arguing, because they don't like to be told by me how to play a hand. I have a sudden ally in the Judge. "This is a very interesting hand," he muses, "because it just feels automatic to duck the first spade. All kinds of good things can happen after the duck—setting up the fourth spade, creating a squeeze situation—but you have to resist the urge to do it, because on this particular hand you can't afford the luxury."

"Hey guys, cheer up." I say. "Think of this: in the old days you all would have made the hand—no problem—because in those days, all we knew about ducks was that they quacked."

No one finds this particularly amusing, except the Bandit, who has his own cute tale about the hand. With the North hand he opened two diamonds, Flannery. The Mona Lisa, with the South hand, jumped to four spades! On the queen of spades lead, all she lost on this hand were two spades and a heart. Making four, for a cool top. Everyone is suitably disgusted by this display of misbidding, and, for once, they commiserate with the Whiner, who is justifiably upset. He, of course, was West, one of the victims.

"Why didn't you lead the king of diamonds?" the Expert asks the Whiner. "Now try making four spades!"

"If declarer plays on a cross-ruff," says the Judge, "I believe she will come to ten tricks."

"See," says the Whiner.

Indigestion

Dinner is over, and I have some observations. Much as I love my friends, and enjoy bridge talk, I do not feel refreshed after this dinner break. In fact, I have acute indigestion. We had a miserable afternoon game, and the punitive postmortems have not cheered me up. On the contrary, all that vigorous rehashing of hands and reliving mistakes have made me quite depressed. I don't believe that I learned one thing from the destructive criticism that went on, ad nauseam. Nor did I enjoy some of those giant egos recounting their great triumphs. My triumphs were few and far between this afternoon, so I resented *their* triumphs. (My honesty in acknowledging this surprises me.) Much of the banter was unkind, and sexist. Am I too sensitive?

I know what hurts most: the rancorous feeling between me and my husband. He's my best friend in the world, my sweetheart, and we're carrying on as if we hate each other.

Solutions to the Dinner-time Dilemma

- If your game was good, and you're on reasonable terms with your husband or wife, then go out with the gang and rehash the hands to your heart's content. The fact that you did well puts some space between you and the postmortems, and you'll probably have a jolly old time enjoying your crazy bridge friends and getting a kick out of *their* mistakes.

- If your game was bad or just merely mediocre, and you're

not feeling especially fond of your partner, then go out on your own, just the two of you, and get away from bridge. Perhaps go to an ice-cream parlor, or exotic dessert place for dinner. Make peace not war. Remember, you have only each other for the evening session.

· Obviously, the bridge will be heavily on your mind, so if you *must* discuss your game, do so in the spirit of examining what went wrong. What led to the bad score on this hand? How can the mistake be avoided in the future? If you genuinely, rationally and unemotionally cannot resolve a hand, put it aside and consult an expert later. Don't go round in circles with it.

· Don't go back to play in the evening session unless you've signed a peace treaty with your partner. You don't want to invite further disaster by starting the evening session in a war zone. If you feel that your differences are irreconcilable on this particular day and it is not a two-session event, go to a movie.

14

Green Shirt, Blue Pants and Man Smoking Behind Pillar: Distractions

♡♡

How to maintain concentration.

"DIRECTOR!" I CALL out, lifting my arm, and fluttering my wrist. My opponents look startled. My husband raises a quizzical eyebrow. "It's your bid," he says.

A distinguished-looking, silver-haired director approaches our table and says to me "Howdy Little Lady. What seems to be the trouble?"

"There's a man smoking behind the pillar," I tell him, motioning to a pillar about 20 feet from us.

"Well, ma'am, I'm not sure what I can do about that," he says to me, waving his hand dismissively.

"Well, for one thing, you could ask him to extinguish his cigarette," I respond sarcastically. "It's only been announced *three* times that this is a no-smoking room." The director mutters, shakes his head, and moves toward the pillar. I get the impression that the "Little Ladies" in *his* life don't cause him this kind of trouble.

"Look, could we play this hand?" my opponent says.

I am holding an uninspiring collection:

♠ 9 3 ♡ 8 6 2 ◊ 9 8 6 5 ♣ A 6 5 3, and I pass.

I see the director talking to the smoker and gesturing at me. They both burst out laughing as the man grinds his cigarette out on the pillar.

"Review please," I say. The auction has proceeded:

Me	North	East	South
Pass	Pass	Pass	1 NT
Pass	2 ♣	Pass	2 ♠
Pass	4 ♠	Pass	Pass
Pass			

I am on lead. I note that they're playing 15-17 point notrumps, and for lack of any inspiration, I table the nine of spades:

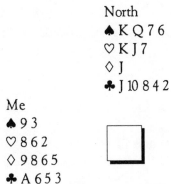

```
              North
              ♠ K Q 7 6
              ♡ K J 7
              ◊ J
              ♣ J 10 8 4 2
Me
♠ 9 3
♡ 8 6 2
◊ 9 8 6 5
♣ A 6 5 3
```

Declarer wins on the board and plays a second round of trumps ending in his hand, while I notice the fall of the jack from my partner. South then plays the king of clubs out of his hand, and since dummy seems loaded with entries, I see no reason to duck. In with the ace of clubs, I think that we'd better cash our heart tricks, so I switch to the two of hearts. It goes jack, queen, ace. Declarer stops to ponder the whole situation, and during the hiatus, I glance across at my husband, who is deep in concentration. He needs a haircut, and has a slightly demented look. With a pang of fondness, I notice that he's wearing his greenie-blue pants with a clashing green shirt. He never notices what he wears, I muse, and yet he always manages to transcend his clothing and look handsome.

Declarer has started to run his tricks: queen of clubs, club to the jack, and the rest of the club suit. He started out with three clubs and throws two diamonds from his hand on dummy's last two clubs. Partner started with a singleton club, and his first two discards are the ten, deuce of diamonds, showing me that he's holding the ace of diamonds. I feel that my pitches are irrelevant, and on the fifth club I throw a heart.

Now declarer starts running his spades, and my partner looks more and more troubled with each passing trick. He is shaking his head. Too late, I start thinking about the hand, and realize that my poor partner is being squeezed in the red suits. He is forced to part with hearts in order to hold onto the ace of diamonds, and declarer wins the last two tricks with the king, seven of hearts. Looking at all four hands, I see that allowing them to make six is going to be a bottom for us.

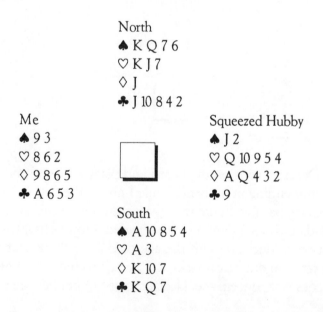

North
♠ K Q 7 6
♡ K J 7
◇ J
♣ J 10 8 4 2

Me
♠ 9 3
♡ 8 6 2
◇ 9 8 6 5
♣ A 6 5 3

Squeezed Hubby
♠ J 2
♡ Q 10 9 5 4
◇ A Q 4 3 2
♣ 9

South
♠ A 10 8 5 4
♡ A 3
◇ K 10 7
♣ K Q 7

Remorse

I notice with regret that I could have held this contract to four if I had led either ace of clubs and a club or a diamond to partner, who would have switched to a club. But I don't fault myself for my lead. Nor do I fault myself for my heart switch. If partner had held the ace-queen of hearts instead of the ace of diamonds and queen of hearts, the heart switch would have been crucial. (Though I probably should have held up on the club ace and waited to see my partner's signal!) What I *do* regret most heartily right now, is that I didn't save my partner from being squeezed, and I could have. Here is the three-card ending that actually occurred (look at me clutching those three useless diamonds!):

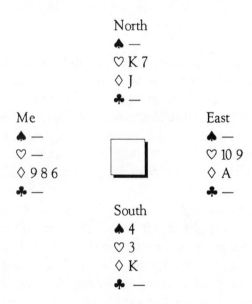

```
                    North
                    ♠ —
                    ♡ K 7
                    ◊ J
                    ♣ —
     Me                              East
     ♠ —            ┌──────┐         ♠ —
     ♡ —            │      │         ♡ 10 9
     ◊ 9 8 6        │      │         ◊ A
     ♣ —            └──────┘         ♣ —
                    South
                    ♠ 4
                    ♡ 3
                    ◊ K
                    ♣ —
```

On the play of the four of spades, dummy pitched the jack of diamonds and East was hopelessly squeezed.

If I had held onto that innocuous-looking 8-6 of hearts, my partner could have pitched down to the stiff ten of hearts with impunity, and my eight of hearts would have taken the 13th trick.

Here is the three-card ending that *should* have occurred:

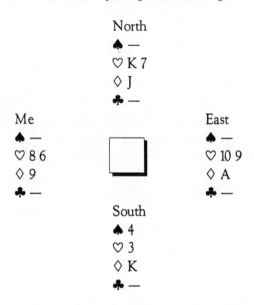

North
♠ —
♡ K 7
◇ J
♣ —

Me
♠ —
♡ 8 6
◇ 9
♣ —

East
♠ —
♡ 10 9
◇ A
♣ —

South
♠ 4
♡ 3
◇ K
♣ —

This is an interesting hand. If the eight and seven of hearts were interchanged, partner would have been squeezed no matter what I kept, and our bottom would have been more honorable. If declarer were clairvoyant, and had not played the *jack* of hearts when I led the two, partner, again, would have been squeezed without my help. If, instead of the two of hearts, I had led the *eight*, "top of nothing," partner would have been genuinely squeezed, too.

The reason this is such a tragedy is that none of these ifs happened! I led the right spot in hearts; declarer *did* play the jack, thereby transferring the menace to my hand, and yet I still let my partner be squeezed by throwing my heart guard.

Ugh! I am so disgusted at myself. During the time when I was thinking about the smoker, the chauvinistic director, my husband's unruly hair and his mismatched clothes, I should have been counting declarer's tricks and visualizing that he had only 11 coming to him: four clubs, five spades and two hearts. My only job on this hand was to save my partner from being squeezed out of his ace of diamonds. Holding onto my two precious hearts would have become obvious if I had followed this train of thought.

Being unnecessarily squeezed or endplayed is my husband's greatest bridge trauma, and I'm not surprised when he berates me mercilessly for my lack of concentration on this hand. I hang my head in misery. For once, he's right.

The Big Picture

In a game where unbroken concentration determines the winners, how does one blot out the world? How can I achieve greatness in bridge when my interest in the game encompasses the whole panorama of the bridge scene, with the endless variety of characters who star in it? When fireworks happen at a nearby table, and a director labors valiantly to douse the flames, I involuntarily tune in. If a husband lurches out of his seat after a bad round, puts his face six inches from his wife's and says "I am checking out of the hotel—I am not going to take this aggravation another minute!" I am there, witnessing the drama. I see the wife respond eloquently, wordlessly elevating her middle finger. I observe a frustrated man in a wheelchair valiantly trying to negotiate his way through the jungle of bunched-up tables and chairs. I wave to my friends. I watch with interest the mountain of female kibitzers surrounding one of my favorite male stars. I see a married friend with his arm around a nubile nymph. Almost involuntarily, these scenes impinge on my consciousness and register in my memory.

The Small Picture

Then there are the immediate distractions present at our own table. As each pair arrives, I observe the attitudes, the shoes, the jewelry, and the handwriting on the convention cards. I notice arthritic hands, and layers of obese flesh spilling over the sides of the chairs.

I pick up on the vibes of the partnership dynamics. I can usually tell whether the pair is having a good game or bad game, and whether they're romantically involved. I can always tell if they're married to each other. Are they rich? Poor? Sick? Students? Republicans? Not that I consciously ask myself these questions—the information simply gets processed as the round proceeds. When, later, we discuss hands in postmortems, I'll hear my husband say something like "He played ace and a heart," and the hand will pop into my head in living technicolor: the portly old woman who played the hand, and all the vivid details about her, from her blue dress down to her matching handbag and high-heeled sandals.

The Marital Picture

Finally, playing with my husband creates the inevitable distractions too. I look at his clothes and notice that his collar is frayed. I see that he needs a button on his sweater. In fact, why is he wearing this sweater when I bought him a new one a month ago? I pick up on his moods, his hostility toward me, or his elation over a hand. I love to watch him planning the play. Sexy. The cozy intimacies during the game distract me too, as do the criticisms after a hand.

Don't misunderstand me. As this hurly-burly of drama and color swirls around us, I am passionately involved in the game—counting cards, figuring distributions, and analyzing declarer's play. Somewhere in my subconscious, all the extraneous stuff is simultaneously registering in my brain. Most of the time, my concentration remains undisturbed, and I play OK, but now and then, the flash of a five-carat diamond arrests me for a split second, and the momentary loss of concentration costs me dearly.

What struck me most when I once kibitzed some world-class players in the Spingold Teams, was not their precise bidding or skillful play. It was that in the midst of a huge crush of kibitzers and a hubbub of noise and activity, they appeared to have removed themselves to a different planet, whose only inhabitants were themselves and their cards. The depth and degree of their concentration were stunning. How I envied them this ability.

How to Improve Concentration

As far as bridge is concerned, the most important thing in

a marriage is good concentration. The harder you concentrate, the fewer mistakes you'll make, which in turn will produce harmony between you and your spouse. If concentrating at bridge is not one of your natural talents, there are many mechanical things that you can do to help focus yourself on the game. I have tried these in recent years, and my game *has* improved because of them.

I find that the period of greatest danger for me and my partner is the first round of an event. There was a time when it seemed that we *always* had a mishap on one of these early boards, because of a lapse in concentration. It was as if we were in a never-never land between the real world and the bridge game, and the cards had not yet engaged our full attention. As the session proceeded, we would acquire a rhythm of concentration, and then it would all become easier.

There are two techniques that we introduced to force ourselves to hone in on the first round.

- Just before the start of the round we remind each other that we have this first-round problem and should make a special effort. This rather simple-minded, trivial-sounding procedure tends to cut off other trains of thought, and starts getting us to concentrate on concentrating.

- As the game is about to begin, I try to withdraw from the table banter or conversation and make my mind go blank. I have a colleague who was once the Tiddly Winks champion of North America. He told me that just before a big game, he would go into a room by himself and meditate. He would empty his mind of everything, breathe deeply, and bring every atom in his body under his control. He could almost *feel* those body atoms slowing down. He found that with his mind focused deeply like this, he could go in and play without being distracted. Obviously, I don't leave the playing area just before the game to slow down my atoms, but I *do* try to withdraw mentally and get my mind under control.

I have found that these last two techniques have helped us significantly in cutting down first-round errors.

Here are some other, unrelated tactics for sharpening up your concentration.

- As declarer, slow down your play by not immediately playing the card you detach. Move it to the end of your hand before putting it on the table. (As a defender, do this mentally.) This skipping a beat gives you a few seconds to reconsider, and sometimes prevents the careless play of a wrong card.

- Go through a mental checklist before playing to the first trick. Here's one I have used as declarer: PDL WDL CESC (piddle widdle cesc).

PDL

P: Points. Has my opponents' bidding told me how their points are likely to be distributed?

D: Distribution. What do I know about it so far?

L: Lead. What does this opening lead tell me? Is it a singleton? Is it reasonable, based on the bidding? (If it is not reasonable, and my opponents are competent players, I'd better think about it.)

WDL

W: Winners. Count your winners.

D: Dummy reversal. Is this the right hand for it?

L: Losers. Count your losers.

CESC

C: Control. Will there be problems maintaining control of this hand? For example, must an ace be knocked out before drawing trumps?

E: Entries. Are there entry problems? Just looking at the cards with this question in mind can change your whole notion of the hand.

S: Squeeze. Are there squeeze possibilities? Do you have to rectify the count?

C: Cross ruff. Is this the right hand for it?

- Use a checklist as defender, too. You must think about points, distribution, winners, losers and entries. Based on what you see in the dummy, predict a logical line of play for declarer. Anticipate the problems he may run into. Can he lose control? Must you cover if he leads an honor in a given suit, or should you duck smoothly? Is this a falsecard situation? Think about all this beforehand, or else you're bound to do the wrong thing.

- Count! Declarer's distribution, partner's distribution, points, trumps, everything. Counting, more than anything else, *forces* you to concentrate! Eventually it may become automatic, but at first, if you don't make a conscious effort to do it, it won't happen on its own.

- If you, as defender, have a weak hand, you have to remind yourself that most or all of the tricks for your side are going to come from your partner's hand. This is where you have to be especially vigilant about concentrating. Can you help partner with your discards? Can you guard any suits in which he is likely to be squeezed?

- Don't discuss bad results immediately following a hand. Especially if you're married to your bridge partner. I've said this before in different contexts: to enable you to survive disasters; to maintain a cool exterior in front of your opponents; to help you stay married. But nowhere is it more crucial than here, in the discussion on concentration. Arguing about hands causes emotional upheavals. Emotional upheavals destroy concentration. And without concentration, you can't play bridge.

15

Ode To Joy: The Long Ride Home

♡ . . . ♡

HOW TO RESOLVE DISPUTES.

WE HAVE TWO types of tapes in our car: pre-tournament, and post-tournament. As we drive to a tourney, the mood is light and breezy. Anticipation fills the car. Happily we discuss Kantar Honor Splits, Colorful Cuebids, or whatever new fandangled device has caught our fancy. All of this to the silken sounds of Arthur Fiedler and the Boston Pops or a Mozart *divertimento*. Life is a melody.

The ride home often requires something with lots of words or crash of drums and cymbals to discourage discussion and drown out unspoken accusations and postmortems. Rex Harrison in *My Fair Lady* screaming "When you let a woman in your life!" or Audrey II, the bloodsucking plant in *Little Shop of Horrors* howling "Feed me!"

· · · · · · · · ·

It is Saturday night and we're driving home after a disastrous day of duplicate. We have a two hour stretch ahead of us, and since we're not speaking to each other, I insert Beethoven's Ninth Symphony into the tape deck and violently punch the volume button. As the familiar chords crash around my head, I try to reconstruct the trauma of today's game.

How the Roof Caved In

Before the start of the session, I had informed my partner that I would not discuss hands during the game, but would note down any hands that I wanted to talk about later. Civilized. I had even attached a blank sheet of paper to my convention card for this purpose. I was, however, willing to converse with him on all other topics—sex education in the schools, the situation in Eastern Europe, and the lovely golf he could have been playing today. We were both in good spirits at the start.

The roof began to cave in somewhere in the middle third of the afternoon. Sitting East in fourth seat, everyone vulnerable, I held ♠ K Q 2 ♡ 8 6 ◊ K J 9 4 ♣ J 10 9 5, and the auction proceeded as follows:

South	West	North	Me
1 ♡	1 ♠	3 ♡	3 ♠
Pass	Pass	4 ♡	Pass
Pass	Pass		

Three hearts was described as a "limit raise."

It was not clear that we should have doubled, but it *was* clear that if they made four hearts we were getting a bottom. My partner led the jack of spades, and when I saw the dummy, I felt quite good about our chances.

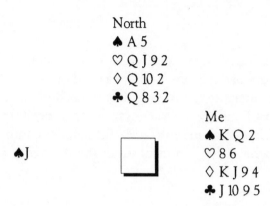

North
♠ A 5
♡ Q J 9 2
◊ Q 10 2
♣ Q 8 3 2

♠ J

Me
♠ K Q 2
♡ 8 6
◊ K J 9 4
♣ J 10 9 5

Declarer ducked the spade-jack lead. Here is what breezed through my ever-hopeful brain as I played the deuce: I don't want to be on lead with this hand. Perhaps partner will switch to a diamond. If he continues a spade, I've lost nothing.

What my unimaginative mind did not anticipate, however, was that my partner would construe the deuce of spades as a suit-preference signal for *clubs.* The next thing I knew was that the genius had placed the king (!) of clubs on the table, causing me to have a temporary loss of pulmonary function. Look at all four hands as you follow the rest of this fiasco.

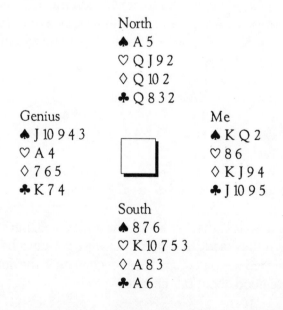

North
♠ A 5
♡ Q J 9 2
◊ Q 10 2
♣ Q 8 3 2

Genius
♠ J 10 9 4 3
♡ A 4
◊ 7 6 5
♣ K 7 4

Me
♠ K Q 2
♡ 8 6
◊ K J 9 4
♣ J 10 9 5

South
♠ 8 7 6
♡ K 10 7 5 3
◊ A 8 3
♣ A 6

Declarer won the club ace, played a spade to the ace and a heart to the king and ace. Partner, perhaps still under the spell of that two of spades, continued with a club. Declarer won on the board, ruffed a club high, ruffed a spade, drew another round of trumps and ruffed dummy's last club, coming down to this position:

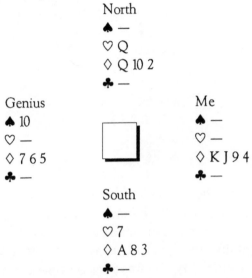

North
♠ —
♡ Q
◇ Q 10 2
♣ —

Genius
♠ 10
♡ —
◇ 7 6 5
♣ —

Me
♠ —
♡ —
◇ K J 9 4
♣ —

South
♠ —
♡ 7
◇ A 8 3
♣ —

A diamond to the ten now cooked my goose. In with the jack of diamonds, I was endplayed up to my ears. Making four!

"There you go again, making unique plays," the genius said tersely. "*No one in this room,* from the weakest to the strongest player, would find the two of spades play on the first trick. I don't understand why you can't play normal bridge and overtake the spade. Now a club, or even a spade return, defeats the contract. Simple defense."

As my temples throbbed at the injustice of it all, I swallowed my retort.

Bd. 6: Jerk! I wrote on my virgin sheet. *Do you think anyone in room would play King of clubs???? Why not use feeble brain to figure I may have only three spades, KQ2? Declarer won't duck with doubleton in both hands! Also, how about diamond switch when in with ace of hearts?*

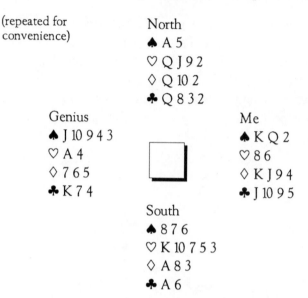

(repeated for
convenience)

North
♠ A 5
♡ Q J 9 2
◊ Q 10 2
♣ Q 8 3 2

Genius
♠ J 10 9 4 3
♡ A 4
◊ 7 6 5
♣ K 7 4

Me
♠ K Q 2
♡ 8 6
◊ K J 9 4
♣ J 10 9 5

South
♠ 8 7 6
♡ K 10 7 5 3
◊ A 8 3
♣ A 6

How like him, I thought, to blame me for a disaster that was (if not totally, at least equally) his fault. The gall! (Several days later, when the air surrounding this hand was less combustible, we agreed that my two of spades was awful, and that his king of clubs was suicidal. My play was poor because it opened up the way for partner to goof, and his play was just as bad because it allowed no recovery if wrong. He was playing me for the A-J-10 of clubs, but should have seen that there was no rush for a club switch.)

Anyway, it was in a most aggrieved state of mind that I arrived at the next round. This time I held:
♠ J 10 9 5 3 2 ♡ 6 2 ◊ A J 7 ♣ Q 6. With no one vulnerable, my partner in first seat opened one club. After a one-heart overcall, I bid one spade. Left-hand opponent bid two hearts and my partner bid two spades. My right-hand opponent now bid four hearts. What should I call?

If my blood pressure had been normal, I believe that I would have hesitated for perhaps two seconds and then passed. This hand was not exactly defense heaven. As it was, with the blood roaring through my veins, my judgement went askew and I doubled. Here were the hands:

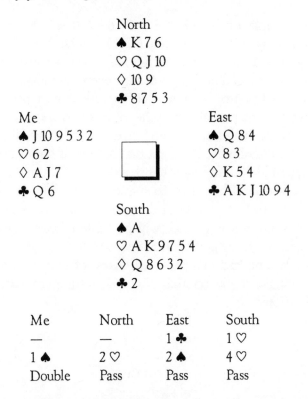

North
♠ K 7 6
♡ Q J 10
◇ 10 9
♣ 8 7 5 3

Me
♠ J 10 9 5 3 2
♡ 6 2
◇ A J 7
♣ Q 6

East
♠ Q 8 4
♡ 8 3
◇ K 5 4
♣ A K J 10 9 4

South
♠ A
♡ A K 9 7 5 4
◇ Q 8 6 3 2
♣ 2

Me	North	East	South
—	—	1 ♣	1 ♡
1 ♠	2 ♡	2 ♠	4 ♡
Double	Pass	Pass	Pass

I led the queen of clubs and we proceeded to take a club and two diamonds—for another bottom.

The tirade was not long in coming. "Here we go again with the absurd doubles," he said, livid with rage. "You have *six* spades and I supported you. How many spade tricks do you think we're going to take?"

Stony exterior. Turbulent interior. I said nothing.

"I don't know why we bother to come," he fumed (one of my favorite phrases of his). I grabbed my paper. *Bd.* 10. *Nor do I,* I wrote.

Another Little Gem
Then, later on, this little gem confronted us. Again with no

one vulnerable, I held ♠ K Q 3 2 ♡ J 6 4 2 ◊ K 7 ♣ K 8 5 . In first seat I opened one notrump (12-14 points). My left-hand opponent doubled and my partner found a two-notrump bid, a sequence we had not discussed in recent memory.

If he had points, he would either redouble or pass, so I decided that he probably had the minors and was inventing a kind of unusual-unusual-two-notrump bid. I was all ready with my three-club call, congratulating myself on my astuteness, when I heard my right-hand opponent bid three hearts. So I passed, and heard three spades on my left. After my partner passed, my right-hand opponent started twitching and squirming and eventually whispered "four hearts." I wasn't surprised when my partner doubled.

By now I had a pretty pessimistic view of all our decisions, and seeing dummy on this one did nothing to raise my expectations.

North
♠ A 10 9 8 7
♡ A 3
◊ A Q 10 4
♣ J 6

Me
♠ K Q 3 2
♡ J 6 4 2
◊ K 7
♣ K 8 5

East
♠ J 5 4
♡ 8
◊ J 8 6 3
♣ A Q 10 9 2

Whisperer
♠ 6
♡ K Q 10 9 7 5
◊ 9 5 2
♣ 7 4 3

Me	North	East	Whisperer
1 NT	Double	2 NT	3 ♡
Pass	3 ♠	Pass	4 ♡
Pass	Pass	Double	Pass
Pass	Pass		

I led the five of clubs to my partner's ace, and, after much grimacing, he returned a club to my king. Now what? It appeared to me that I possibly had a natural trump trick, and therefore the king of spades seemed right. Declarer won the ace of spades, ruffed a spade (ugh!), ruffed a club (ugh!), ruffed a spade, finessed the queen of diamonds (ugh!) and cashed the ace of diamonds dropping my king. Here is what was left:

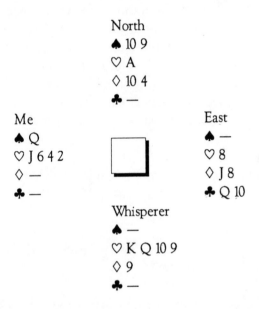

North
♠ 10 9
♡ A
◊ 10 4
♣ —

Me
♠ Q
♡ J 6 4 2
◊ —
♣ —

East
♠ —
♡ 8
◊ J 8
♣ Q 10

Whisperer
♠ —
♡ K Q 10 9
◊ 9
♣ —

Declarer cashed dummy's ace of hearts, ruffed a spade to his hand and cashed the king, queen of hearts. My jack of hearts won the thirteenth trick, as my partner's jack of diamonds just evaporated. Declarer had fallen into one of these fortuitous situations in which he was able to telescope his two losers into one, while we collected yet another bottom. Boy, were we ever in Rock Bottom City!

If he attacks me on this one, I'm going to kill him, I thought calmly. I flinched as he stretched across the table and appropriated my cards for a long, sour-faced perusal. I know him so well. This was his telltale sign that he was rethinking his own defense. I also rethought, and furiously scribbled on my sheet.

Bd. 22: 2N moronic bid. If pass like bridge player, they'll settle in 3H. Defense moronic too. Return heart at trick 2 and declarer loses 3 clubs plus a diamond. Obvious!! K of diamonds not in your hand, so where are our tricks coming from??

(Small victory note: He agreed with me about a week later. Not on the two notrump bid, but on the defense.)

To continue a description of this game would be to write an endless litany of acrimonious encounters. My partner's anger and frustration at my plays unleashed themselves bitterly all day, and, after a while, I ceased to care about the bridge. I started to earn the criticism. Eventually I stopped writing on my piece of paper, since all this suppressed conversation was giving me writer's cramp.

Ode To Joy

So here we are in the car, more than halfway home, when Beethoven's fourth movement, *Ode To Joy*, in all its glory, bursts upon us.

♪♫ *O Freunde, nicht diese one! Sondern lasst uns angenehmere anstimmen und freudenvollere!**

Amidst all this Power and Beauty, I am a quivering jellyfish of imperfections. My bridge life is floating before my eyes. It is more than I can bear. I put my head in my hands and sob.

The effect is startling and immediate: he swerves the car and pulls off the road. Away from the bridge table he still loves me, and awkwardly he embraces my sobbing head. But I am inconsolable.

"Nothing I do is right anymore," I cry. "It's as if I've lost the ability to play. You pick on me every hand."

"It's because you never seem to make normal plays," he answers in his defense. "It drives me crazy."

**O Friends, no more these sounds! Let us sing more cheerful songs, more full of joy!*

"But often it's *your* plays that are wrong. So why am *I* the one always taking the rap at the table?" I demand. He doesn't reply, and Beethoven fills the void.

"I've become too nervous to play bridge," I hiccup eventually, "Not because I'm afraid I'll make mistakes, but because I may do something that makes you unhappy. You know, something that incurs your wrath!"

"Hey. Maybe we'd do better if, before you played a card, you asked yourself *What play would make him happy?* Huh? Huh? How about it? I bet if you had used the *What-play-would-make-him-happy?* test you wouldn't have played that two of spades this afternoon!"

This is us, then, the Tragedy Queen and the Buffoon. Wordlessly we wend our way home. The black atmosphere has lifted somewhat, and has been replaced by mild depression. Beethoven's joyful message continues on low volume. Next event. Another day.

. . . .

There was a time, many moons ago, when bridge did not cause this kind of strife in our lives. When the game was over, it was no big deal. We drove home like any normal couple, who had just been to a normal activity, like a movie.

No more. We are now at a stage in our bridge evolution where we both think we know absolutely everything. We are highly opinionated and *very* sensitive to criticism. This is a Serious Endeavor, like being business partners, or circus partners, and friction is inevitable. No question. It comes with the territory. What *is* in question is the manner of settling the disputes. Can we do it in a way that strengthens the partnership, or are we firmly set on a path of destruction?

How to Resolve the Conflicts

Unfortunately, the gap between what *should* happen and what *does* happen is as wide as the Grand Canyon:

- Ideally, you should have a perfect game in which no conflicts arise, and then drive home in joyful harmony. *What actually occurs, is that the game is dreadful, you blew a match, you threw the event and you hate each other.*

- The drive home, this interlude between Bridge and Real Life, should be used to let off some of the steam that has built all day. You should take this chance to open the valves. *Actually, you drive home in murderous silence, like two pressure cookers simmering and about to boil over.*

- Turn the stereo down low so that you can hear each other and have a meaningful discussion about what went wrong. *We put it on top volume, with crashing chords to drown one another out.*

- Since you're going to make up eventually, do it sooner rather than later. *You sulk the whole way home, enter the house not on speaking terms, and let the unpleasantness spill over into your lives over the next several days.*

- Don't postpone the inevitable argument. Have it out now, in the privacy of your car. *Save the fight for when you get home, so you can wake the children and feel guilty all week.*

- Let the drive home be a period of "constructive fighting," a time to air your grievances and tell your partner what has upset you/hurt you/thrown you or confused you. *Say dreadful, destructive things that come back to haunt you when the bridge itself is long forgotten.*

- It's OK to say things like Let's not play such-and-such anymore, it's causing too many foul-ups. Not *You bid like a lobotomized baboon.*

- I'm angry because you blame me every time we misdefend

a hand. *You are ugly/stupid/revolting, and I deeply regret being married to you.*

- I was furious that you accused me of not concentrating when I took a reasonable line that didn't work. *I realize now that I don't love you anymore. In fact, what did I see in you in the first place?*

- I am so frustrated because you cannot resist the urge to discuss a hand after a disaster. *I'm going to start looking for another husband/wife/lover/mistress/bridge partner.*

- I would be so happy if you behaved like we were on the same side. This constant tug of war wears me down. *Everytime I look at your face I want to throw up. Like now.*

- I wish you would listen to some of these things that I say over and over again. These arguments are becoming tedious. *I want a divorce.*

You don't have to walk into the house holding hands. But you should try to be, if not the best of friends, at least on minimally amicable terms, when you park the car. Here is the bottom line: Destructive name-calling, swearing and insults, good as they may feel at the time, do not lead to a swift resumption of good feeling. They leave a bad taste in the mouth. They chip away at the marriage. And they dull your enthusiasm for the next bridge game.

16

Only a Game: Mid-life Crisis

HOW TO ACCEPT THAT "WORLD CHAMPIONS"
IS NOT PART OF OUR FUTURE RÉSUMÉ.

I AM STANDING in line at T-Shirts Are Us, patiently waiting to have my T-shirt personalized. In the spirit of announcing special carding at each table, I have decided, for a lark, to emblazon

WE PLAY
LAVINTHAL
DISCARDS

on my chest in large, sparkled, neon letters.

Finally it is my turn, and the woman behind me and I watch in fascination as each letter is painstakingly pressed on with a hot iron. Eventually, the woman cannot stand it a second longer and says, "I have to know what your T-shirt means."

"It's a term used in bridge," I explain. "You know, the, uh, card game?" Her face lights up.

"Gee," she says, "I also play bridge, but in my game, ace is four, king is three, queen is two. . . ."

Later I reflect on the difference between her game and my game: Mine is a third of my life.

Bridge Dreams

I am dreaming that I am a bridge player, cleverly disguised as a wife, mother and teacher. Bridge has percolated through all my layers, and I cannot escape.

My children want quality time and I teach them bridge.

My husband wants love and attention, and I whisper sweet bridge nothings at him.

My math students demand, "How will we use all this in Life?" and I haul out my calculations from the other night and show them that six diamonds *was* a reasonable slam.

My computer programming class learns how to generate random bridge hands—reams of them—which I then take home to bid with my beleaguered bridge partner.

In Peter Shaffer's play, *Amadeus*, when Salieri stretches out his arms and howls in grief and frustration, "Come to me, for I am the God of Mediocrity!" my soul bursts forth onto the stage and embraces him, as I mourn my hopes and dreams as a bridge player.

How To Be Happy

Several years ago, just before my 40th birthday, I found myself in the library on the day following a dismal bridge tournament. In the New Books section I espied a catchy title, something prosaic, like *How to be Happy*. The title beckoned, and before long the book and I were together in a little coffee shop down the road.

If you have reached mid-life or beyond, the book intoned ominously, you have come to a point where you must confront the reality of your abilities, and reassess your goals for the future. For some it means facing the fact that the career heights envisioned in youth are unattainable. For others, the insight that their chosen path in life has not brought fulfillment.

This is a time to accept your limitations. A time to adjust your plans accordingly. If you are unable to carry out this process of self-examination, the book warned, you will never know happiness again. Because being happy depends on accepting and living with who you *are*, not hankering after who you'd like to be.

The Dread Plateau

Reading that book marked a turning point in my bridge aspirations. Slowly, painfully, I confronted the disillusionment, the fact that we were no longer up-and-coming players scaling great heights, but middle-aged plodders on a vast plateau. Wryly I cheered myself up with two thoughts: the plateau was higher than that reached by most bridge players, and at least it was a plateau and not a downhill slope! Sadly, I acknowledged that "World Champions" was not part of our future résumé.

. . . .

We are playing in a large Regional Pairs event, blazing a trail of glory. Finally, after many weeks of unsuccessful bridge, we are in contention.

Sitting South, with no one vulnerable, I pick up the following hand: ♠ A 10 7 ♡ 10 8 4 ◇ K 3 ♣ A K 7 4 3.

Here is how the bidding proceeds:

Me	West	North	East
1 ♣	3 ◊	Double	Pass
3 ♠	Pass	4 ♠	Pass
Pass	Pass		

My partner's double was negative, showing hearts and spades. There was a time that I would have bid a rosy three notrump with my meager K-x of diamonds, but at least my bridge longevity has taught me the futility of such bids! So I settle on my better major, and, rather unhappily, bid three spades. Partner, slightly flushed at the prospect of a major victory, drives on to four. The opening lead is the ace of diamonds, and I find myself staring at a difficult play hand, one in which it looks very easy to lose four tricks!

Dummy
♠ J 8 4 3 2
♡ A K 7 2
◊ Q 2
♣ J 10

☐

Me
♠ A 10 7
♡ 10 8 4
◊ K 3
♣ A K 7 4 3

The first thought that strikes me as I survey the dummy is that I am in an ambitious contract, one that probably won't be reached by at least half of this Open-Pairs field. Therefore, if I make it, we're sure to get close to a top score, and if not . . . well, I don't even want to think about it.

My second thought is that the key to this hand is how to play the trump suit for just one loser, because if I lose two trumps, I'm going down if the clubs don't behave perfectly. Dolefully I stare at the trump combination and conclude that my only hope is a low spade to the ten, followed by cashing the ace. This will work whenever East has the K-Q, K-Q-x, K-x or Q-x of spades.

Anyway, after all these ruminations, I play the diamond king under the ace, and win the diamond continuation on the board. I play a spade to the ten, East following with the five, and West wins the queen. Now my only hope, I think, is that West started with Q-x-x of spades, and my ace will drop her partner's king. Gloomily, I notice that this is very unlikely, since my left-hand opponent advertised a long diamond suit with her preempt.

After a while, West shifts to a low heart. I win with the ace of hearts and lead the jack of clubs. I see that more trouble looms for me—the clubs must be brought in to take care of heart losers, and I'm not exactly loaded with entries to my hand. The finesse is certainly better odds than a 3-3 split, so I play low on the jack of clubs, but West wins the queen. For someone who preempted, she sure has been on lead a lot, I think bitterly. Another heart comes back. I win on the board and cash the ten of clubs, everyone following. I know for sure now that I cannot make the hand. West simply doesn't have room in her hand for three spades.

I return to my hand with the ace of spades, and, as expected, the king does not appear from East's hand. I run my clubs, discarding dummy's two small hearts and eventually go down one. All in all, I lose a diamond, a club and two trumps.

"I guess we got too high," I say, unhappily. "My hand wasn't that great."

"Your hand was fine, and the bidding was fine," my partner says evenly, "but your handling of the spade spots was not so great."

My curiosity overcomes my irritation at him, and his words set me thinking again about the hand.

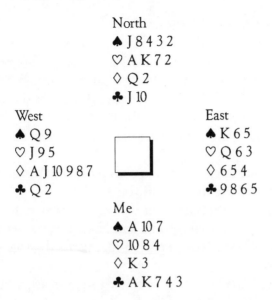

North
♠ J 8 4 3 2
♡ A K 7 2
◊ Q 2
♣ J 10

West
♠ Q 9
♡ J 9 5
◊ A J 10 9 8 7
♣ Q 2

East
♠ K 6 5
♡ Q 6 3
◊ 6 5 4
♣ 9 8 6 5

Me
♠ A 10 7
♡ 10 8 4
◊ K 3
♣ A K 7 4 3

I take another careful look at the spade suit, and then I see it! Once the ten of spades lost to the queen, I should have led the *jack* from dummy, hoping to pin the nine. West was much more likely to have Q-9 than Q-x-x. Of course! I had analyzed that West was unlikely to have three spades, yet I had failed to act on it!

It is all so simple and obvious now that I am filled with anguish and self-disgust. How is it possible, that someone who has been playing bridge this long, and at this level, could miss this suit combination? I simply did not *see* the extra chance of Q-9 of spades in West's hand. Oh misery. Oh frustration. The euphoria of the evening has been dispelled by this one hand.

This particular card combination is forever branded on my brain, but I see now that there will always be others that elude me. This, then, is yet another nail in the coffin of my bridge hopes.

"I'm sorry," I whisper to my partner, "I blew it for us."

We were third in the event. . . .

. . . .

A Touch of Mental Illness

The Great Inner Devil of Mid-life Depression and the Great Inner Therapist of Mid-life Peace square off for possession of my sanity. As the Devil tries to suck me into the abyss, the Therapist soothes me by rationalizing away my shortcomings, and assuring me that I am still a worthwhile human being.

Therapist: "You were third in a major event. Hey! That's not bad!"

Devil (chuckling): "You don't understand. At your age, there's winning and losing, and you just lost."

Me: "Why is it that the older we get, the more hurtful the mistakes? Why was that terrible hand like a mortal wound?"

Therapist: "Look. No one plays bridge perfectly. That's part of the allure."

Devil: "It hurts because you think you're smart, when, in fact, during the execution of this hand, you were pretty dumb."

Therapist: "It hurts because being a Good Bridge Player is part of your definition, along with Good Parents, Successful Careers and Happily Married. Malfunctions in any of those departments—bad days at work or lousy bridge sessions—all attack the foundations of who you are."

Devil: "Have you considered changing your definition and taking up something new, like tennis?"

Therapist: "Don't even think it! At this stage of your life, the last thing you need is group tennis for beginners. Stick with bridge. It's what you do well."

Devil: "Know why you're sore? You're a middle-aged bridge player with a bruised ego. Those vultures you call bridge friends are waiting to pick you apart if you play like a turkey."

Therapist: "Notice that these problems are worse if you're married to your bridge partner, because over the years you have spent hours together on improving your game."

Devil: "Have spent a fortune on each masterpoint!"

Therapist: "Have acquired an impressive bridge library."

Devil: "Have raised two bridge orphans!"

Therapist: "Have had hours of bridge-related joy."

Devil: "Have had hours of bridge-related aging!"

Therapist: "Have tasted victory, the killer. Now there's no going back."

Devil: "Do you notice how your husband's tolerance has dwindled? That man never was a paragon of patience, but nowadays even the smallest errors from either one of you translate into huge upsurges of vitriolic feeling. Maybe you need to face the fact that occasional flashes of brilliance are the best that you can hope for. Look at you! While the normal middle-aged world is toying with hair restorer, face lifts, new lovers, and new spouses, you are into Mid-life Bridge Trauma. By the way—have you considered new *bridge* partners??"

17

Separate Beds: The Breakup

♡   . . .♡

HOW TO SAVE THE MARRIAGE.

A tragedy in three acts

Act One

The Scene: A large Ballroom at the Buffalo Regional.

The Time: Mid-afternoon, July 4th. (No picnic.)

The Exact Place: A single table near the exit.

The Players: The usual protagonists, Me and Him, sitting North-South, plus another husband-wife pair, who look a bit like Jack Spratt and his wife.

The Exact Moment: Two seconds after the sixth round. A sloppy defense has just occurred at the table.

Jack Spratt: *To his partner, with just the right patronizing air.* Well played, darling!

Me: *Aside.* Lassie could have played it well, the way we defended.

Him: *To me, shaking that once gorgeous head.* When declarer got round to playing the heart suit, you should already have had an accurate count of my diamonds.

Me: *Irritated.* Why rely on me to be a counting genius, when you yourself could have cashed the setting trick?

Him: *Frustrated.* Because at that stage it would have been premature.

Jack: *Rising.* Honey, I'm going to get some coffee. Want some?

Wife: No thanks, sweetness. But how about a Danish?

Me: *With an exaggerated frown of puzzlement.* Premature? We already had three tricks in the bag. Premature?? Why, I think it was long overdue!

Wife: Ha ha!

Him: *A little too loudly.* You know it's sad. Your bridge is so hopeless, that you have to resort to stupid remarks. *He gets up and roughly shoves back his chair.* I'm going for a break!

Me: *To his retreating back.* While you're at it, why don't you join the National Association for the Humor Impaired?

Wife: *Leaning towards me conspiratorially.* I see you also have one that walks on water. [CURTAIN.]

Act Two

The Scene: Same Miserable Tournament.

The Time: Mid-evening, July 4th. (Many fireworks.)

The Exact Moment: The start of a new round.

The Players: The two central tragic figures, still North-South. Sitting West is a friendly elderly lady. Sitting East is a nice, earnest young man, perhaps her son.

The Atmosphere: Tense.

The Vulnerability: Favorable.

My Hand: ♠ A 5 4 ♡ A 10 9 8 ◇ Q 4 ♣ A 6 4 3.

The Bidding:

Nice Lady	Me	Nice Man	Him
—	—	Pass	2 ♠
Pass	2 NT	Pass	3 ◇
Double	3 ♠	Double	Pass
Pass	Pass		

The Explanation: Two notrump was an enquiry asking him to clarify his hand. The three-diamond response showed a bad hand. It did not necessarily deny a feature, and it gave no further information about the length of the spade suit. Three clubs would have shown a good hand with a five-card spade suit; three hearts, a good hand with a six-card spade suit and a club feature; three spades, the same with a diamond feature; three notrump the same with a heart feature or specifically A-K-Q-x-x-x of spades.

The Full Deal:

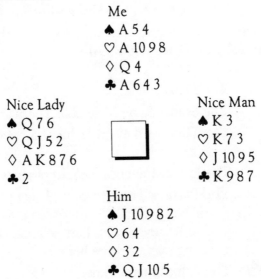

```
                    Me
                    ♠ A 5 4
                    ♡ A 10 9 8
                    ◇ Q 4
                    ♣ A 6 4 3
Nice Lady                             Nice Man
♠ Q 7 6                               ♠ K 3
♡ Q J 5 2                             ♡ K 7 3
◇ A K 8 7 6                           ◇ J 10 9 5
♣ 2                                   ♣ K 9 8 7
                    Him
                    ♠ J 10 9 8 2
                    ♡ 6 4
                    ◇ 3 2
                    ♣ Q J 10 5
```

The Opening Lead: The king of diamonds.

Him: *Visibly agitated upon seeing dummy.* You are out of your mind! How could you bid with that garbage?

Me: *Aside.* Uh oh. I think we're in trouble. He must have a subminimum this time. *To him.* You can't seriously expect me to pass with this hand?

Him: *Shaking with fury.* You sabotage every bid I make.

Me: *With bile rising at his unreasonable attack.* Why don't you just be quiet and play the hand!

Lady: *Shifting her chair back one inch to avoid the fumes.* Please!

Young Man: *Looking very pained.* Yes, please!

The Play: The Lady cashes the king, ace of diamonds, as her partner, East, follows high low. She now switches smoothly to the two of clubs, and her partner wins the king, as my partner, equally smoothly, drops the queen.

Young Man: *Aside. With furrowed brow.* Oh no, what now? A heart looks dangerous. A trump looks helpful for South. A club looks hopeless because he doesn't have any. Ergo, a diamond!

The Play, Continued: Partner eyes East's jack of diamonds with ill-concealed incredulity. No longer is he facing a two-trick set. On the diamond he pitches a heart, as he ruffs in dummy. He plays ace of hearts and ruffs a heart, and is in his hand to lead the jack of spades.

Lady: *Aside.* I think I'll cover.

(Two minutes later, after South has claimed, making three doubled.)

Him: *With unpleasant face leaning toward me.* Don't you see that if you simply pass we will get to play two spades, undoubled? Whereas if I pass originally, West will open one diamond, and they will reach two or three diamonds, their perfect spot. You have to be careful when I've opened at that vulnerability.

Lady: *Looking distressed.* I think, dear, that you didn't have enough to double.

Me: *Glaring at him with unrestrained fury.* I can come up with one thousand weak two-spade hands in which *game* will make opposite my hand, and several thousand more where *three* is cold. I'm not clairvoyant—I can't tell when you've decided to open with nothing but *%#@!#* in your hand!

Young Man: *Looking downcast.* Perhaps if you hadn't covered the jack of spades. . . .

Him: *With exasperated hand-flinging gesture.* You don't have a bid! Change your queen of diamonds to the queen of hearts, and then, *maybe.* . . .

Me: That's it. I've had it with you.

Young Man: *Looking baffled.* Did I miss something, or did you guys just get a top??

Greek Chorus:

> Oh, fine irony!
> The breakup occurs
> Over a hand
> On which they got
> A top.

[CURTAIN.]

Act Three

The Time: After midnight, that same night.

The Place: A hotel room, one of those large impersonal rooms with two double beds and framed pictures of someone's farm on the walls.

The Scene: The room is crowded. Hatred, full-bodied, in black shining armor, dominates the scene. Anger, red and fiery, stomps about, burning brightly. Misery, snivelling weasel, roams unfettered. Fear creeps along the edges. Love, a thin, malnourished waif, cowers behind the cobwebs on the wall. Reason lurks in the shadows. The Greek

Chorus, ghosts of past and present bridge tragedies, are everywhere.

(The hero of the action is already in bed, reading *A Tax Guide For College Teachers*. The heroine, with murder in her heart, is hurling clothes and accusations in all directions.)

Anger: *Hissing at occupant of bed.* I misplay. He takes wrong views. I misdefend. He makes imaginative switches that don't work. I overbid. He takes reasonable risks. When he psyches and I compound matters with a close call, the disaster somehow always ends up being my fault.

Greek Chorus:
Can't accuse them
Of being wired.

Hatred: *Knocking aside the tax book.* Don't underestimate me! Feel my power. I am pure unsullied crystallized venom.

Greek Chorus:
Many years ago, a man playing with his wife,
Ducked an ace.
She had ducked the king on that same trick.
The next trick crashed the ace upon the king.
He later said he would have killed his wife
If he had had a gun.

Me: This was shocking to me then. But now I understand.

Hatred: Hit him! Throw your convention cards at him. He's vulnerable in that bed.

Reason: Don't do it. You're civilized.

Me: I hate Him! I don't want to be in this room with him. I want to leave him. I want to take the children to another state. I want to take a lover. My capacity for wanting to hurt him is infinite.

Love: *In a whisper.* I am filled with horror at the intensity of this reaction, over—what?—his unjustified criticism of a bid?

Reason: It's not just that. It's cumulative.

Me: How is it possible that we've come to this?

Fear: Don't do something you'll regret. Come to bed and sleep on it.

Misery: *Sobbing.* This psychological beating—I feel like a battered wife.

Him: *Upset.* What a thing to say. Let's go to sleep.

Hatred: Not in the same bed, surely? The thought of being near him. . . .

Love: *Rushing from the room.* Oh no! Not separate beds!

Greek Chorus:

> Buffeted by the cruel vicissitudes of Bridge
> Scarred by the symbolic act of separate beds
> At dawn's first light they make a grave decision.
> Dissolve the bridge partnership. Save the marriage!

> (Love limps back in. Bruised. Older. Sadder. Wiser.)

Greek Chorus: And now to a new era . . . [CURTAIN.]

END OF PLAY.

18

Extramarital Bridge: After the Breakup

♠♡   ♡♣

IS BRIDGE WITH OTHER PARTNERS
THE ONLY WAY TO GO?

THE DEMISE OF our bridge partnership is treated with shock, boredom, glee or disbelief, depending on whom we talk to.

"How will you *manage?*" my mother gasps.

"It's only *bridge,* Ma," I assure her. "Everything else is intact."

"When Dad and I stopped playing together, it was downhill from there," she says dolefully.

My children are delighted. "Does this mean we get some peace?" the older one asks.

"No, silly, they don't have to be actually *partners* to fight about bridge," the baby replies with great wisdom.

"Now I get to steal you as a partner," our friend, the Bandit, says to me.

"She's yours," my husband responds.

"And I can finally play with *you*," the Lunatic says to my husband.

"You deserve each other," I say.

Henry and Selena are horrified. If this calamity can befall us, the Rocks of Gibraltar, can they be far behind?

Our friend, the Expert, as usual has it all analyzed: "You should have done this years ago," he tells us breezily. "A pushy woman in a husband-wife partnership is a disaster."

Our dear friend, the Judge, says, "You watch. The ink will barely be dry on your new partners' convention cards before you're opposite each other at the bridge table again." To my husband he adds: "You'll miss her craziness." (Does he mean my flair?)

In a burst of bad taste, a bridge acquaintance sends us one of those *Too-bad-you-got-divorced* cards. On the inside it says *Think of it this way: Today is the first day of the rest of your life.*

· · · · · · · · ·

And so it begins, the endless merry-go-round of finding other partners. There's no shortage of offers—I feel that we're basking in the novelty of being the new kids on the block. We play with quite an assortment of partners, and then have a jolly old time complaining about them, together, afterward. What fun to join forces, for a change, for some wicked postmortems!

The jury, however, is still out on the breakup as a permanent solution. In those early weeks, in the first flush of "freedom," I ask myself: What do I want in a bridge partner? I think I want a tolerant, respectful, pleasant, non-smoker with a sense of humor. How misguided can one get?

I Miss Bidding With Him

The first thing that I miss is our bidding system with its little bag of tricks and gadgets. Take the Gambling Three Notrump, for example. Here's a little gem that has been part of our system for so long that I can't even remember where we stumbled upon it. When partner opens three notrump, showing a long solid minor, a bid of four diamonds asks partner to cuebid a singleton or void. A response by opener of four notrump shows shortness in the other minor, while five clubs or five diamonds denies any singletons or voids. It never comes up, of course, but it's so comforting just to have it there, in case. . . .

· · · · · · · · ·

It is Saturday night. We are playing rubber bridge at home, with friends Donald and Joan. They are good friends and good players who have also occasionally been known to raise the roof with their marital bridge mishaps. They were therefore happy to play men versus the women for a change. Joan and I are losing heavily, mainly due to rotten cards. The men are being royal pains in the neck, lording it over us, as if their winning was just as natural as day follows night.

With everyone vulnerable, I pick up

♠ A K 4 ♡ A K Q ◇ 8 7 6 2 ♣ 9 8 7.

My partner, the dealer, opens three notrump, gambling, which we agreed would show a long, solid minor and no outside ace or king in this position. My heart leaps into my throat. Here it is, finally, the perfect hand on which to trot out the four-diamond bid asking about singletons or voids, and, just my luck, I'm with the wrong partner! I do the best I can under the circumstances and bid five clubs. This is not matchpoints, after all. My partner's hand hits the table with exactly the holding I feared. We have missed a cold six:

North
♠ 5 2
♡ 7 4 3
◇ 4
♣ A K Q J 6 4 3

☐

Me
♠ A K 4
♡ A K Q
◇ 8 7 6 2
♣ 9 8 7

The lovely little four-diamond gadget would have gotten us there, easy as pie. Over three notrump a four-diamond bid would elicit a four-notrump response from partner, showing either a stiff diamond or stiff club. Now I could happily bid six clubs, which partner would correct if her suit were diamonds.

It takes me one minute to lay down the hand and write down the relatively puny score. I am so disappointed. I feel, irrationally, as if something has been stolen from me.

"Come on girls, *bid* those cards instead of complaining about them," Donald taunts. I catch my husband's eye, and he gives me a rueful shrug. Sigh.

I Miss Playing With Him

One night I make a date to play with a young hotshot player at our club. He arrives at the last minute with a stunning girlfriend in tow. Miss World. My heart sinks. She is going to distract us both. I know it.

"Mind if she watches?" he asks.

"Not at all," I lie. "She may bring us luck."

In the precious two minutes in which we might have discussed bidding methods, my partner fusses at the coffee table and emerges triumphant with steaming hot chocolate for his companion. I watch with a jaundiced eye as she settles in next to him, one slender leg lightly brushing his, her head on his shoulder. "Perhaps you'd be more comfortable on his lap?" my subconscious offers.

The first few hands are routine, nothing much to comment about. I am declarer in some of them, and my partner, as he plays the dummy, goes into reclining mode, and flips the cards up with his left hand while he strokes Miss World's knee with the other.

Then suddenly I am holding:

♠ A J 10 8 6 4 3 ♡ 2 ◇ K 9 6 5 2 ♣ —.

I open one spade, and my partner bids two hearts, which, in the one second before the game, we agreed to play as game forcing. I would love to bid three diamonds, but 20 years of grief have chastened me and I say a quiet two spades. Lover Boy has taken his right hand off Miss World and is studying his cards intently. Three diamonds, he says! I breathe evenly and raise to four diamonds. Four notrump, he says! I respond five diamonds, hoping that we play normal Blackwood, and my partner shrinks a tad as I say it. Five hearts, he continues. I assume he wants to play it there, but six diamonds seems indicated at this point, and I bid it.

West	Me	East	Lover Boy
Pass	1 ♠	Pass	2 ♡
Pass	2 ♠	Pass	3 ◇
Pass	4 ◇	Pass	4 NT
Pass	5 ◇	Pass	5 ♡
Pass	6 ◇	Pass	Pass
Pass			

The opening lead of the ace of clubs is viewed by everyone with interest. My partner looks relieved to see it, and he leans back, swinging in his chair, as he contemplates the hand. He ruffs the club on the board and leads a low diamond. When East throws a club, the consternation is evident on my partner's face—the hand is not going to be as easy as he thought. He goes into the tank for an eternity, and I see a flash of brilliant rhinestones as his kibitzer tries to ease the tension by massaging his neck. Come to think of it, my neck could do with a little something, too.

Here are the North-South hands:

Me
♠ A J 10 8 6 4 3
♡ 2
◊ K 9 6 5 2
♣ —

Lover Boy
♠ Q
♡ K Q J 9 8
◊ A Q 7 4
♣ K Q 8

Eventually South cashes the king of clubs, pitching the two of hearts, followed by the ace of spades and a spade ruff. Everybody follows, but the king doesn't fall. The sad situation is this: West has three trumps left, and South is running out. Enough said. Eventually he loses control and goes down two.

"*C'est la vie,*" says my partner, the hotshot, smiling at me ruefully. Then he buries his face in Miss World's neck, muttering "Don't ever play this game, sweetheart, it's too hard for you."

As for me, I am hopping mad. Yes, I know that the hand was a bear once the trumps didn't break. Still, all that neck and knee action sure as heck did nothing to point his thoughts in the right direction! Couldn't he *see* that dummy had entry problems?

Later, when I take a good look at this hand, I see that declarer got into trouble because he failed to realize that he didn't have enough trumps in dummy to ruff a club, draw a round of trumps, ruff himself back to dummy to ruff the second round of spades, ruff himself back to dummy again to ruff out the king of spades, and then *return* to dummy to enjoy the spades!

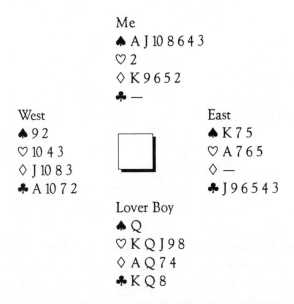

Me
♠ A J 10 8 6 4 3
♡ 2
♢ K 9 6 5 2
♣ —

West
♠ 9 2
♡ 10 4 3
♢ J 10 8 3
♣ A 10 7 2

East
♠ K 7 5
♡ A 7 6 5
♢ —
♣ J 9 6 5 4 3

Lover Boy
♠ Q
♡ K Q J 9 8
♢ A Q 7 4
♣ K Q 8

His line would have worked if either East or West had held king-singleton or king-doubleton of spades, which is less than half of the time.

The right line, therefore, seems to point to a spade finesse, which will work half of the time. Notice that running the queen doesn't help either, because you then need to ruff yourself to dummy (leaving two trumps there) to ruff one more spade.

The best hope then for making this hand goes like this: Ruff the opening club lead and play a trump to the ace. On receiving the bad news, cash the club king, throwing the two of hearts from dummy and play the queen of spades to the ace, followed by the jack of spades. If East plays low, cross your fingers and let it ride. If it holds, *you're still in dummy* to lead another spade. Here is the position at this stage:

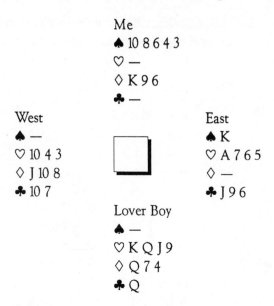

Me
♠ 10 8 6 4 3
♡ —
◊ K 9 6
♣ —

West
♠ —
♡ 10 4 3
◊ J 10 8
♣ 10 7

East
♠ K
♡ A 7 6 5
◊ —
♣ J 9 6

Lover Boy
♠ —
♡ K Q J 9
◊ Q 7 4
♣ Q

When you play another spade from dummy and ruff it low, West cannot defeat you. If he overruffs and returns a heart, you can ruff in dummy and draw his last two trumps, ending in dummy to enjoy those luscious spades. If he does not overruff, you draw two rounds of trumps (leaving one of his trumps outstanding) and run the spades. West can ruff anytime—the small trump in dummy is the entry to those good spades.

Would my husband have made this hand at the table? Maybe. Maybe not. But he sure would have had both his hands and his head in the right place: on the cards!

I Miss Defending With Him

I eye my latest partner for the evening with misgivings. He's youngish, paunchy and has a cherubic face that smiles at me often for no good reason. He also has a disconcerting habit of scratching his head violently every time he tries to think, sending little snowstorms of dandruff onto his shoulders.

He's a visitor from out of town, and the manager of our club, aware of my newly acquired single bridge status has arranged the date. "He's a good player," she tells me. My husband has a date with one of the club regulars, so I am happy to accept.

An aspect of bridge that has never occurred to me before, is the amount of time you spend simply *looking* at your partner. How depressing if the sight is unappetizing. You are cruel and hypocritical, I chastise myself. Why am I dwelling on my partner's looks and idiosyncrasies when my mind should be on bridge?

Somewhere in the middle of the evening, playing against a wily old bird, I pick up ♠ K J 10 9 3 ♡ K J 8 2 ◊ K ♣ K 5 2.

The auction, with no one vulnerable, proceeds as follows:

Wily Bird	Me	North	Dandruff
1 ◊	1 ♠	2 ◊	Pass
3 NT	Pass	Pass	Pass

I lead the two of hearts, and hope swells in my breast at the sight of the anemic dummy.

North
♠ 8 5 4
♡ 7 5
◊ J 9 8 3 2
♣ Q J 7

Me
♠ K J 10 9 3
♡ K J 8 2
◊ K
♣ K 5 2

The wily bird goes into a long huddle before calling for a low heart from dummy. Partner wins the ace of hearts and declarer contributes the three. My partner plays the piano on his head for a brief moment, then switches to the seven of spades. Declarer ducks, and I find myself in with the nine. That's two tricks for us. I later come to the conclusion that my best defense at this stage would have been to exit with the king of diamonds, but at the time I don't see it that way. I decide to continue with hearts and to sit back and wait for my other kings to materialize as tricks.

I duly cash the king of hearts, on which partner plays the nine, and declarer the four. I then exit with the eight of hearts and am gratified to see partner's ten on this trick, as South wins the queen in his hand and pitches a spade from dummy.

After another huddle, declarer, with no quick entries to dummy, plays the ace of diamonds, and acknowledges my falling king with a satisfied grunt. He now runs three more diamonds, on which partner pitches three clubs, and I discard a club followed by the ten of spades, then the three of spades, leaving this position:

North
♠ 8
♡ —
♢ J
♣ Q J 7

Me
♠ K J
♡ J
♢ —
♣ K 5

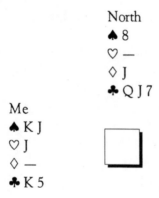

South cashes the ace of clubs, and cocks his head at me unconsciously, as he tries to reconstruct my hand. I'm in trouble. I will have to nonchalantly stiff my king of spades on the play of the last diamond. If I carelessly ditch the thirteenth heart, South will throw me in with the king of clubs, and I will be endplayed. My only hope is that declarer will think that I started with six spades, 6-3-1-3 distribution, that my jack of spades was a falsecard concealing the six, and that he will throw me in with the king of clubs anyway. Triumphantly I will then cash the jack of hearts, the setting trick.

South is shaking his craggy head and ruffling his feathers. He has no clues as to who holds that diabolical jack of hearts. Partner's play of the nine then the ten of hearts may well mean he has the jack. With a sigh he leads the last diamond to the board, and, in tempo, I part with the jack of spades.

My partner, who, during the hiatus, had apparently lost interest in the hand, now begins to think. My heart starts sinking as he unleashes a shower of flakes onto his collar. Is he going to torpedo my defense? The answer is not long in coming. Before my horrified eyes, he places the six of spades on the table (a dagger in my heart) and all is lost. Declarer has seen all the spades except the king, and it is a simple matter for him to cash the ace-queen of spades to make his contract.

"Oh, well played," my cheerful partner beams at declarer. He is blissfully unaware of my subtle spade discards and the turmoil in my breast, as he beams at me, too.

Here is the hand in its entirety:

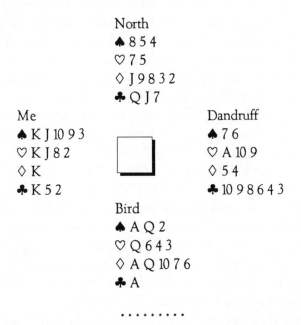

North
♠ 8 5 4
♡ 7 5
♢ J 9 8 3 2
♣ Q J 7

Me
♠ K J 10 9 3
♡ K J 8 2
♢ K
♣ K 5 2

Dandruff
♠ 7 6
♡ A 10 9
♢ 5 4
♣ 10 9 8 6 4 3

Bird
♠ A Q 2
♡ Q 6 4 3
♢ A Q 10 7 6
♣ A

· · · · · · · · · ·

How I relish telling this story to my husband later on, complete with embellishments and pantomime. We laugh heartily at my poor partner's expense. He really was very nice. Later, in a more sober mood, I perceive that my husband, with all his faults and foibles, would have been the first to appreciate my play, and the last to sabotage it. He would not, however, have beamed at me throughout the evening!

. . . .

For several weeks now I've been playing with a variety of other players. I have been dropped in cuebids, dropped in Blackwood and dropped in the Grand Slam Force. I have signed off and my partners have bid to the moon. I have wanted count when my partners gave attitude, and suit-preference when my partners gave count. I could now write a treatise on the various meanings of high-low. I have become entangled in more mixed signals these past few weeks than in my entire married life.

And, yes, I have been free of the psychological tensions inherent in playing with my husband. Oh, the partners I have had who smiled at me as they blundered, laughed with me as they imaginatively booted tricks and joked with me as they went down in cold contracts. It is now shockingly obvious to me that what I miss most about my husband is his thoughtfulness as a bridge player. Surprise! That deep and wonderful concentration, more often than not leading to the right decision. I think sadly of the countless times I urged him to "lighten up" or "have more fun." Meaning—what? Despite all my "fun" partners of the past few weeks, I've not had much fun. I've missed the intricacies of our bidding system, well-honed over the years, and the satisfaction of getting to the right contract because of something we discussed together. I've missed the discipline of careful, long-discussed carding, the joy of a tough defense accurately executed. My husband and I have built up a lifetime of bridge understandings. How sad that we were unable to make it all work for us.

More than I care to admit, I've missed the intimacies. The special look when something worked. His unique eyeball roll as he put down a less than robust dummy. His surreptitious wink when he was about to make a doubled contract.

Heavens. I can't believe that I've missed his *sexiness* at the bridge table! His incredibly cool, collected, slender good looks. His furrowed brow. His crisp intelligence.

Wait a minute, I tell myself sternly. Don't go soft in the head. Before you swoon from all this nostalgia, let me remind you about the dreadful tension that he generated when you played with him! Surely you haven't forgotten that? No, I concede, I haven't. But I wish that I could somehow have moderated it and harnessed it to my advantage. I'm beginning to believe that his high expectations somehow spurred me to play better. Oh my perverse nature! Is Erma Bombeck really correct that the grass is always greener over the septic tank?

· · · · · · · · ·

My bridge priorities have been turned on their heads.

· · · · · · · · ·

I have become a traitor to my own cause: I'm beginning to think that it's more important to have a good partner than a pleasant one.

· · · · · · · · ·

Pinch me, am I awake?

· · · · · · · · ·

In short, I want him back.

19

Happily Ever After: Together Again

♡♡

WHAT MUST CHANGE TO MAKE IT WORK
THIS TIME AROUND?

AN OLD ACQUAINTANCE unexpectedly drops into town and asks me to fix him up with a bridge partner. "Here's what I need in a partner," he says. "If he's male, then he must be very good." I raise one eyebrow. "Ye-e-e-s?" I say.

"If she's female," he continues, "Her bridge ability should at least be inversely proportional to her looks. If I have to spend the evening watching someone trump my tricks, let her at least be gorgeous."

"And I suppose if she's *really* bad bridge-wise, she'd better be gorgeous *and* single?" I offer sweetly.

"You always were a smart gal," he tells me.

He then goes on to add cheerfully that he's actually willing to forego all of these requirements to play with either one of us! But, equally cheerfully, I inform him that we're not available.

Believe it or not, we're back together again at the bridge table . . .

. . . .

Playing with different partners has not been the great bridge renewal we'd hoped for; so we're happy to join forces yet again. For my part I'm thrilled. But don't get me wrong—this is not going to end with soft violin music in the background as we happily ride off to a regional in the sunset.

Let us at least go back to our local club one more time to see how things will be different the second time around . . .

A Second Honeymoon It's Not
The club is holding a round-robin team game, always a popular event. At the start of the game, while many pairs are filling out convention cards, I start filling out an index card—not with our conventions, but with a list of my husband's attributes as a bridge partner. I want to keep this handy for when the going gets tough. And tough it will get—I have no illusions about that.

. . . .

On the fifth board of the first match we are defending a two-spade contract. I lead a low heart from Q-x-x and am happy to see partner's king hold the trick. There are three small hearts on the board, so it looks likely that we can take three heart tricks on this hand. Instead of cashing them, however, at trick two my partner switches to the ace of diamonds. I have three to the ten in this suit and dummy has jack fourth. I signal vigorously with the ten of diamonds—upside down attitude—trying to tell my partner that I hate his switch and could we please take our heart tricks? Despite my violent signal—we've agreed, in principle, to *never* use tens for signaling—partner continues with the deuce of diamonds and declarer wins the king. He now takes a losing trump finesse and I find myself in for the second time. My gut feeling tells me to cash our hearts, but I decide to trust my partner and I play a third diamond for him to ruff. He fails to ruff and the world swims. Not only does he not ruff, he starts muttering and shaking his head. Oh, and declarer ends up making an overtrick in a contract that we should have held to two.

So here it is, the classic friction situation: my husband is obviously unhappy with my defense, while I know for sure that the fault is his. What must I do about it to enable us to continue with a workable bridge partnership and a reasonably happy life?

The one thing I've learned for sure is that to have a big pow-wow at the table is futile. We might as well kiss that match and the partnership good-bye. So here is what I actually do. Even though every fiber of my body is screaming INJUSTICE, I pretend that nothing unusual has happened. I act as though I'm unaware of his unhappiness. I do not move one muscle in my face. Calmly I take my cards out of the next board and adjust my spectacles. I bid.

We proceed to have two good boards and everything appears to be back to normal. Tonight when we get home, we will discuss the contentious board.

When we compare scores with our teammates we find that they have murdered our opponents, and we win this match by a landslide. Our little partscore misadventure, luckily, slips into obscurity.

The second match goes smoothly and I'm all pumped up when we bid a close slam using a convention that we discussed earlier. We win this match, too.

In the third match we get to defend a vulnerable three notrump and have to find discards as declarer runs her long suit. I'm in the hapless position of not knowing which suit to guard. It transpires that I discard the wrong suit, and in fact should have taken an inference and *known* that it was the wrong suit. My error hands this unmakeable contract to my opponents. A disaster.

My husband, who has promised to try and tone down his

criticism at the table, cannot restrain himself. He does not share his thoughts with the whole room, which he might have done in the past, but he does say, softly, to me, "That was unbelievable. What were you thinking about?" I am not unaware of my defensive error and apologize swiftly. This is the only conversation I'm willing to have on this particular hand at this particular moment. "How could you not blah blah blah?" he continues. Puzzled, concerned, but not overly aggressive. Still, I am done. As far as I'm concerned the discussion at the table is over. I will not defend my plays, nor will I try to explain my thinking or lack of it. I will be silent.

You may be wondering what has changed. We're not exactly having a second honeymoon here. Well, for one thing, I've decided to give serious thought to the kinds of things I do to detonate him at the table. Here are my New-Era Resolutions:

- I shall no longer be a rosy optimist when evaluating my hands. In this spirit I shall pass more and go down less. Example: Holding ♠ A J 7 6 2 ♡ 9 2 ◊ 8 ♣ A 8 6 4 3, when my right-hand opponent opens two hearts (weak), I shall pass rather than overcall two spades. (On the actual hand, during the Old Era, we ended up in five diamonds doubled, going for 500.)

- I shall no longer be Merlin the Magician when defending at matchpoints. This means that I will cease to conjure up magic holdings in my partner's hand. More often than not, in the old regime, the Merlin principle led to overtricks, rather than undertricks, for declarer.

- Even if every vibe at the table tells me that a particular opponent holds a missing honor, I shall make the percentage play and win in the postmortem. I shall stick to our partnership agreements as if my life depended on it.

My husband, for his part, is not the list-maker that I am. He is, however, willing to agree to a few general principles. He will try to control the hostility when I make a play that he *perceives* as wrong. (He concedes that his snap analyses are occasionally wrong, and do not do much to enhance our game.) He finds it very difficult to avoid hand discussion at the table, but making a *huge effort* to curtail this will be his major contribution to maintaining partnership harmony. He definitely will try to stay in his chair at all times and not go flying through the roof when I provoke him—not even when it's justified. In other words, he will try to conform to normal standards of civilized behavior.

For me the major difference in the New Era is that the penny has finally dropped: he is *not* going to change—not significantly. If I want to continue to play bridge with him, which I really do, I have to accept that he will continue to criticize me after a hand and *I* must change my responses to him. Making me feel good about myself is not one of his strong suits as a partner. He doesn't stroke me when I play well, nor does he spare me when I go wrong. Nor is he willing to wait before pointing out my errors. Nor is he forthcoming about *his* mistakes. No matter how much I rant and rave, and accuse him of not loving me, these things are not going to change. This then, is my hope: If at least one of us does not talk bridge at the table, the table talk *will* eventually be lessened. This will then lead to a calmer partnership atmosphere, more conducive to accurate bridge.

You may be puzzled by my tremendous motivation in wanting this to work. Well, he comes as a package deal so to speak. As I sit and seethe with anger, after he's criticized my defense, I haul out my index card and remind myself why I wanted him back:

- Most of the time he's a terrific bridge player. He's by far my best partner. (Main reason.)

· I love our bidding system.

· It's convenient to have a built-in bridge partner. (Don't knock it. In my busy life I don't have time to be constantly arranging dates.)

· He's willing to drive to bridge tournaments in bad weather. (Non-trivial.)

· He's a sexy, good-looking guy, my best friend, and I'd rather be with him than with anyone else. (Crazy, huh?)

On the last board of the disastrous three-notrump match, he doesn't like the line of play I took on a hand. "Surely it would have been better to ruff the spade early?" he says to me in his new reasonable tone. In response I take out my copy of *Bridge Today* and start reading Zia's hilarious article on bridge and romance. I'm free! I am not going to discuss bridge at the table anymore. As I heard a foreign gentleman on TV saying just the other night, "It takes two to make tango."

· · · · · · · · ·

It is the last match of the evening. I'm feeling encouraged, because things are looking up in the partnership department. In the past hour my partner has cut down on the discussions— he doesn't like talking to himself—and we've had some great hands.

On the last board of this very close match, with neither side vulnerable, I pick up in first seat:

♠ K 10 7 ♡ 5 3 2 ◇ 8 6 3 ♣ K Q 10 4.

I pass and hear the following auction:

West	Me	East	Him
—	Pass	Pass	1 ♣
1 ◇	2 ♣	Pass	2 NT
Pass	?		

I decide to bid the game, not only on the strength of my club holding but because we need good result. Also, I have every confidence in his declarer play! The opening lead is the two of diamonds and these are the hands:

Dummy (Me)
♠ K 10 7
♡ 5 3 2
♢ 8 6 3
♣ K Q 10 4

♢ 2   □

Declarer (Him)
♠ A 5 4 2
♡ K 6
♢ A Q 4
♣ A 9 8 2

My partner peers at the dummy and rocks back and forth on his chair like some ancient rabbi. The opening lead goes to East's king and partner wins the ace. He now runs his clubs, discovering that West started with J-6-3. On the run of the clubs, East throws two spades and West throws the ten of hearts.

Declarer now plays the ace-king of spades and West throws the eight of hearts on the second spade. A predatory gleam appears in my dear husband's eye as he now plays the queen of diamonds followed by a diamond. West can cash his three good diamonds but is then endplayed in hearts. Our ninth trick is the king of hearts. "Well played!" I say—"Well bid!" *he* says—and this time we do both crack a smile.

When we return to compare scores, we discover that this hand wins the match for us. All of the hands were pushes, except for this last board. At their table, the North-South players failed to reach the game, when North passed South in his 15-17 one-notrump opening. South made only two.

We pull out the cards and compare the play:

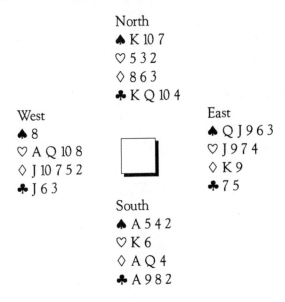

North
- ♠ K 10 7
- ♡ 5 3 2
- ◇ 8 6 3
- ♣ K Q 10 4

West
- ♠ 8
- ♡ A Q 10 8
- ◇ J 10 7 5 2
- ♣ J 6 3

East
- ♠ Q J 9 6 3
- ♡ J 9 7 4
- ◇ K 9
- ♣ 7 5

South
- ♠ A 5 4 2
- ♡ K 6
- ◇ A Q 4
- ♣ A 9 8 2

The lead was also the two of diamonds, and at trick two declarer ducked a spade. He wanted to do this early, he later explained to his partner, to discourage a heart switch from East. He had decided early on that a 3-3 spade break was his best hope for making overtricks in this contract. And when East won the spade, he *did* in fact continue with a diamond.

The play now continued identically. When the spades failed to break, however, and South threw West in with a diamond, West could now cash three diamonds and the ace of hearts as before, holding the contract to two.

My husband tells our teammates that as soon as East showed up with the king of diamonds, he placed West with the ace of hearts. "What else could he have for his bid? I also decided that to bid one diamond with a crummy jack-fifth suit probably meant that he was short in one of the black suits. Luckily it was spades and I could strip the hand and throw him in."

As they babble on happily, I think about our partnership. This hand is a typical example of why I want to keep him as a partner. He thinks deeply about the hands. His analyses extend beyond the superficiality of playing for unlikely 3-3 breaks. He's not always right, but he's always thoughtful.

Our bridge future together is uncertain, but for now, I'll enjoy the glow of our recent success. Despite the guff that we both dish out in dollops, my hopes are high that we can make the partnership and the marriage work—simultaneously. For better or for worse.

If you enjoyed "How to Play Bridge With Your Spouse *and Survive,"*
you might wish to consider
one or more of the other
fine publications by
Granovetter Books.

♣

Granovetter Books
Publishers of Bridge Today
18 Village View Bluff
Ballston Lake, NY 12019
(518) 899-6670

➤ Books published by Granovetter Books:

I Shot My Bridge Partner by Matthew Granovetter	$12.95
Murder at the Bridge Table by Matthew Granovetter	$12.95
Tops and Bottoms by Pamela & M. Granovetter	$11.95
Spingold Challenge by Allan Falk	$11.95
Bridging the Gap by J. Peter Kichline	$ 9.95
The Best of Eddie Kantar	$13.95
Bridge is a Partnership Game by Roth & Stone	$13.95
The 1,001 Workbook by Frank Stewart	$14.95
Roman Keycard Blackwood by Eddie Kantar	$ 8.98
Picture Bidding by Al Roth	$19.95
The Bridge Today Wall Calendar	$ 9.95

Bridge Today magazine edited by The Granovetters
$24 for one year (6 issues — bi-monthly)

Send check and mail to:

Granovetter Books
18 Village View Bluff
Ballston Lake NY 12019

Or phone: 1-800-872-2081
fax: 518 899-7254

Major credit cards accepted.

085)

5

Bridge Today Magazine

Individual back issues are available for $7 each.
One-Year Bridge Today Subscriptions: $24 per gift.
Subscriptions make great gifts!
The recipient gets the current issue and a festive gift card
with your compliments.

1 Year = $24 *

2 Years = $44 *

3 Years = $59 *

* Canadians add $5 per year.
Overseas add $8 per year.
U.S. Funds.

We accept MasterCard, Visa and American Express

 1-800-872-2081

LIFE-TIME SUBSCRIPTIONS

Due to popular demand, we are now offering Life-Time Bridge Today Subscriptions at $500. Life-Time Library Subscriptions are still available at $1,000 — includes your magazine plus 6 featured books each year.

December Gifts: All December holiday gifts that are so specified will be mailed on Dec. 1st. [Orders mailed directly to you will always be shipped out immediately.] For UPS delivery, please add $2 per address. Please add appropriate sales tax for New York destinations. Canadians: Please add $5 per subscription (per year) and $1 per book. Overseas: Please add $8 per subscription (per year) and $1 per book. All orders payable in *U.S. dollars only.*

HOW TO ORDER BRIDGE TODAY

$24/year

In N. America, phone toll-free:
1 800 872 - 2081

Fax: 518 899-7254

CANADA: By credit card or check; $29/yr — U.S. funds (includes VAT)

OVERSEAS: By credit card ($32/yr) to Bridge Today's offices in America. Include your phone number and credit card expiration date. Airmail is $44/yr.

LIFETIME: $1,000 library; $500 magazine.

The 1992 Bridge Today Wall Calendar
{Legends Edition}

Each month includes:

• a legendary player's drawing with his or her most memorable hand.

$9.95

Makes a great gift!!

• all holidays and National bridge schedules listed on dates, with plenty of room to write your own schedules.

• famous bridge players' birthdays.

188

"A brash newcomer enters the field of periodicals."
—Alan Truscott, New York Times

Bridge Today is America's fastest growing bridge magazine. The first issue appeared in July, 1988. The magazine is designed for everyone who plays bridge and is the only bridge publication to emphasize not only the technical side of bridge, but the human element. The writers do not give lectures; instead they write as if speaking to the reader in a conversation. In addition to the regular columns,

Bridge Today presents tournament reports by the participants rather than by third-party anyalysts. Our writers reveal their own thoughts and emotions as they actually happened in the heat of battle! You'll find plenty of quizzes, photographs, contests, humor, book excerpts, and a Book Shop which offers to subscribers a 25% special discount on a featured book in every issue.

"The writing style of the various super-star contributors is extremely entertaining and the content is valuable."
—Ted Horning, Toronto Star

Bridge Today includes regular exclusive features by Eddie Kantar, Alfred Sheinwold, Mike Lawrence, Jan and Chip Martel, Eric Kokish, Martin Hoffman, Al Roth, Zia, Terence Reese, Kit Woolsey, Ernst

Theimer, Marty Bergen and Matthew & Pamela Granovetter. Thus America's cream-of-the-crop is represented, together with internationally famous superstars from London, Montreal and Pakistan.

"This magazine will make your mouth water."
—David Ezekial, Mid-Ocean News

Bridge Today appears in a convenient 6 by 9 inch format on a non-glossy smooth surface with easy-to-read 10-point type face—exactly like the type on this slightly smaller and less-smooth page.

Bridge Today costs $5.50 per issue, but only $24 per year for six issues. Here, for your inspection, is a replica of the Table of Contents page from the September/October 1991 issue:

Sample Table of Contents: September/October 1991

BRIDGE TODAY

♠
♡
♢
♣

Volume 4 Number 2 Editors: Pamela and Matthew Granovetter

Full coverage of the Bridge Today All-Star Game in the November/December issue

Bridge Today is published six times a year by Granovetter Books - 18 Village View Bluff, Ballston Lake, NY 12019. ©
1991 Granovetter Books. All rights reserved. Reproduction in whole or in part without permission is prohibited. Second-
Class Postage rates are approved at Ballston Lake, NY and additional mailing offices. ISSN number: 1043-6383. **Post-
master:** Send address changes to: Bridge Today - 18 Village View Bluff - Ballston Lake, NY 12019. Editors: Pamela and
Matthew Granovetter. Technical consultants: Estee Griffin and Robert W. Nichols. Rates: $5 per issue or $24 per year.
Canada: add $5 U.S. funds. Outside N. America: add $8 surface, $20 airmail, U.S. funds only.

190

Order Form for Bridge Today Magazine

Bridge Today Subscriptions   *New, Renewal, Gifts*

Name _____

Address _____

City/State/Zip _____

Check Box: ☐ 1 Year ....$24 *   Method of Payment:
             ☐ 2 Years............$44 *   ☐ Check Enclosed
             ☐ 3 Years............$59 *   ☐ Credit Card

Credit Card Type: ☐ Master Card
                    ☐ Visa
                    ☐ Amex

Name of Credit Card Holder: _____

Credit Card #: _____ Expires _____

Send a gift-subscription of Bridge Today to:

Recipient _____

Address _____

City/State/Zip _____

Check one:
          ☐ 1 year   ☐ 2 years   ☐ 3 years

Mail to: Bridge Today • 18 Village View Bluff • Box F • Ballston Lake NY 12019
Phone: 1-800-872-2081 or fax 1-518-899-7254

*In Canada, add $5 per year. Overseas, add $8 surface or $20 airmail per year.

ORDER FORM FOR BOOKS

Your Name: _____

Address: _____

City/State/Zip: _____

Please send directly to me:

Item	Quantity	Price	Total

Credit card number: _____   Exp. _____

Name of card holder: _____

Total cost to my address (add $3 per address for postage): $_____

Please send these gifts directly to the recipient.

    Item(s):
    Name
    Address
    City/State/Zip
    Sign card:

                    Total cost (add $3 for postage): $_____

                    Tax (NY destinations): $_____

                            Sub total: $_____

                        Total enclosed: $_____

Please write additional orders on separate paper and mail to:

Bridge Today, 18 Village View Bluff, Ballston Lake, NY, 12019.

Or phone 1-800-872-2081. Master Card, Visa, and Amex accepted.

Checks payable to: "Bridge Today."

Order Form for Bridge Today Magazine

Bridge Today Subscriptions   *New, Renewal, Gifts*

Name _____

Address _____

City/State/Zip _____

Check Box: ☐ 1 Year ....$24 *   Method of Payment:
             ☐ 2 Years............$44 *   ☐ Check Enclosed
             ☐ 3 Years............$59 *   ☐ Credit Card

Credit Card Type: ☐ Master Card
                    ☐ Visa
                    ☐ Amex

Name of Credit Card Holder: _____

Credit Card #: _____ Expires _____

Send a gift-subscription of Bridge Today to:

Recipient _____

Address _____

City/State/Zip _____

Check one:
              ☐ 1 year   ☐ 2 years   ☐ 3 years

Mail to: Bridge Today • 18 Village View Bluff • Box F • Ballston Lake NY 12019
Phone: 1-800-872-2081 or fax 1-518-899-7254

*In Canada, add $5 per year. Overseas, add $8 surface or $20 airmail per year.